The Miser of Middlegate

The Miser of Middlegate

Carolyn Gray

The Miser of Middlegate
first published 2014 by
Scirocco Drama
An imprint of J. Gordon Shillingford Publishing Inc.
© 2014 Carolyn Gray

Scirocco Drama Editor: Glenda MacFarlane
Cover design by Terry Gallagher/Doowah Design Inc.
Author photo by Leif Norman
Printed and bound in Canada on 100% post-consumer recycled paper.

We acknowledge the financial support of the Manitoba Arts Council and The Canada
Council for the Arts for our publishing program.

Library and Archives Canada Cataloguing in Publication

Gray, Carolyn, 1966-, author
    The miser of Middlegate / Carolyn Gray.

A play.
ISBN 978-1-897289-96-9 (pbk.)

    I. Title.

PS8613.R387M57 2014   C812'.6   C2013-906490-7

J. Gordon Shillingford Publishing
P.O. Box 86, RPO Corydon Avenue, Winnipeg, MB Canada R3M 3S3

For Graham Ashmore and Krista Jackson

Characters

Winchell .... the Miser

Mia .... wife of Winchell, mother of Emily

Emily .... their daughter

Richard .... butler to Winchell, friend to Emily

Martin/Waiter .... the love interest

Acknowledgements

Special thanks to Jean-Baptiste Poquelin, Alan Williams, Allan Hudson Gray, Matthew Handscombe, Rory Runnells, Patricia "B.F." Hunter, Erin McGrath, Jay Brazeau, Ardith Boxall, Rea Kavanagh, John B. Lowe, Amber Casselman, Angie St. Mars, the Manitoba Arts Council, the Winnipeg Arts Council, Sydney Coopland, Mikaela Wight and Casey Shapira.

The author would also like to acknowledge Nick Rice, Marina Stephenson Kerr, Shannon Guile, Andrew Cecon, and Ryan James Miller for their significant input into the development of the script.

Production History

The Miser of Middlegate was first produced by zone 41/Theatre Projects Manitoba, Winnipeg, and premiered on October 3, 2013, with the following cast:

WINCHELL..Nicholas Rice

MIA...Marina Stephenson Kerr

EMILY ....Shannon Guile

MARTIN/WAITER... Andrew Cecon

RICHARD ....Ryan James Miller

Directed by Krista Jackson

Set Design by Grant Guy

Costume Design by Angela Fey

Lighting Design by Scott Henderson

Sound Design by Greg Lowe

Dramaturge: Bruce McManus

Production Manager: Steven Vande Vyvere

Production Consultant: Hugh Conacher

Apprentice Stage Manager: Ali Fulmyk

Aprrentice Dramaturge: Casey Shapira

Carolyn Gray

Carolyn Gray is a writer, actor, director, designer, educator, and puppeteer. Carolyn won the Manitoba Day Award for her play *The Elmwood Visitation* (Scirocco Drama, 2007), and also won the John Hirsch Most Promising Manitoba Writer 2008 award. She is also the author of *North Main Gothic* (Scirocco Drama, 2010). *The Miser of Middlegate* is the final play of Carolyn's Winnipeg trilogy. She is a founding member of Adhere and Deny Object Puppet Theatre founded by Grant Guy. A new book documents the company: *Open Fragments: The Theatre of Adhere and Deny* (Lives of Dogs Press). Carolyn has a particular interest in independent theatre, original plays, and rural Canada.

Act I

Scene 1

MIA and WINCHELL, basking in the afterglow of a delicious boozy anniversary meal.

MIA: Thirty-seven years. You haven't changed a bit. *(Aside.)* More's the pity.

WINCHELL: Thirty-seven years. And look at you, just a few laugh lines. *(Aside.)* Her face looks like a creme brûlée after the first whack of the spoon.

MIA: Do you remember when eating in a restaurant like this, never mind ordering wine and dessert, was a pipe dream?

WINCHELL: The mark-up here is criminal. This bottle of wine— at least 150%. The steaks 600%.

MIA: How we bought our food on Friday night, cooked on the weekend, and lived off the same dish all week?

WINCHELL: This pork belly and white bean appetizer—a good big pork belly is $7 in Chinatown. 800% mark-up. Soup—1000% at least—at least!

MIA: Remember the hamburger and noodle casserole I used to make? Shudder.

WINCHELL: Dessert—piddly serving.

MIA: People say 'hand to mouth' but we were literally hand to mouth when we first married. When god forbid you need an aspirin and you've run out because it's just not in the budget.

WINCHELL: Then you borrow two aspirin off your neighbour and you do the same to the neighbour on the other side and the acquaintance on the street, and so on, and soon, you have a free bottle of aspirin.

MIA: Winchell, you've always been full of solutions, I'll hand it to you.

WINCHELL: And you always argued, but I was always right. Admit it. We wouldn't be where we are today without me.

MIA: It's true, we wouldn't be where we are today without your…attention to detail. Better known as your stingy—

WINCHELL: Shh… Keep on like this and it'll be all your fault if the waiter overhears and expects a big tip.

MIA: He's picked the wrong table for that, hasn't he, Winch?

WINCHELL: I don't hand over money for nothing.

MIA: It's such a marvellous story, like a fairy tale, how we succeeded.

WINCHELL: Let's not trip too far down memory lane.

MIA: God! You're afraid someone's going to overhear that we have money!

WINCHELL: Quiet! You're drunk.

MIA: The thing is, people might look at us, see the cut of my clothes, see that you're with me, and imagine we don't have a care in the world—but they don't understand that money just doesn't drop out of the sky. How we clawed our way up. Do you remember how your mother used to save money by putting a bowl on your head to cut your hair? And when she passed on you tried to get me to do the same but I refused—and then you tried to cut your own. Disaster. You were furious when you were reduced to going to the barber.

WINCHELL: Good god, that's right, mother did give me a bowl cut.

MIA: You looked just like Ringo back then.

WINCHELL: I did, didn't I?

MIA: You were so happy when you finally went bald.

WINCHELL: That's technically a monthly savings that I don't need a haircut now, isn't it?

MIA: No, you're bald.

WINCHELL: But I don't need a haircut so it's a savings, right?

MIA: Well, in sense it is a savings. I guess.

> WINCHELL takes out a little black notebook and begins notating.

WINCHELL: What other things do you remember from the past?

MIA: Winch, reminiscing? That's not like you.

WINCHELL: You remember better. Tell me. About how we were thrifty.

MIA: Thrifty memories. OK… Remember in the old days I used to make our clothes?

WINCHELL: Yes! You think—

MIA: Dream on. And we made almost all the renos on our first café ourselves—with the help of library books.

WINCHELL: That's right, we did!

MIA: We couldn't spare a dime.

WINCHELL: What a savings!

MIA: We did well.

WINCHELL: Another, Mia. Another about how we saved money.

MIA: Oh, Winchell, for god's sake. How about when we first met, coffee was a nickel.

WINCHELL: That's bittersweet, because now we get $2.75 a cup in our cafés.

MIA: True.

                 They toast.

             When we met, I was in that little boarding house on McMillan with a shared bathroom.

WINCHELL: It was cheap.

MIA: And horrible.

WINCHELL: But you moved out on your own nonetheless.

MIA: You know I had to get away from my family. For the sake of my dignity, I wanted new money, not old. And I wanted to make it myself. In my life—only you've respected the entrepeneur in me.

WINCHELL: You moved out of your comfortable childhood home, you forewent security and luxury for the sake of your dignity as a young woman…

MIA: Just a second, Winch…

WINCHELL: You wanted to stand on your own two feet—

MIA: I'm not kicking our daughter out.

WINCHELL: I didn't suggest we kick her out.

MIA: Good. Because that would mean trouble between us.

WINCHELL: God forbid, Mia. But it is time to start charging her rent.

MIA: Oh, not this again!

WINCHELL: Yes, again! She's just turned twenty-one.

MIA: But you've been trying to charge her rent since she was fourteen.

WINCHELL: But I didn't succeed, did I?

MIA: And every year since then!

WINCHELL: We both worked since our teens, and yet our daughter—

MIA: I've heard this before.

WINCHELL: And you'll hear it again. She needs to pay rent now, I insist. It will put the fear of god into her and get her up and working.

MIA: Oh, you're intolerable.

WINCHELL: But you know I'm right.

MIA: What is the point of all this money if we can't enjoy it?

WINCHELL: I fail to see how our daughter lounging on her duff is enjoying our money.

MIA: Grrrr. Fine, fine, I hate this, but I suppose as she's 21, a nominal rent then.

WINCHELL: She's seen reason!

MIA: Don't push it. You really know how to spoil things. It's a rare gift you have.

WINCHELL: I am her father.

MIA: The funny thing about you, Winch, is that your circumstances have changed, but *you* never change. It's like, duh, something's missing in your brain. I get being tight when you're poor but being tight when you're rich—

WINCHELL: Keep your voice down about our money—

MIA: I'll speak as I please.

WINCHELL: You're tight too, and just as often, but a different variety of tight.

MIA: You drive me to it.

WINCHELL: Likewise. If I wasn't watching the funds—

MIA: You can't take it with you.

WINCHELL: Perhaps when you're done buying more clothes and jewels and handbags, you could buy yourself a little sobriety.

MIA: You're right. I have done everything wrong, trying to buy myself a little fun.

WINCHELL: True fun cannot be bought, my dear.

MIA: I've said you're right, Winchell.

> *MIA slips the gift certificate out of an anniversary card, which she props up on the table jadedly, and puts it in the bill folder.*

Don't forget to leave the tip we agreed upon. I'm serious, Winch. Where's the bathroom? Excuse me.

> *MIA goes to the washroom. WINCHELL fiddles with the bill folder. WAITER (MARTIN) drops a paper bag off to WINCHELL and picks up the bill folder.*

WAITER: Any change, sir?

WINCHELL: No, no.

> *MARTIN goes to leave.*

Just a second there, not so fast. Come back here. Yes, yes, yes, right back here while I check this over. I want a witness.

MARTIN: *(Aside.)* I've never come across a bigger asshole in all my years as a waiter—and that's saying a lot. I'll give him something to check over. But could he handle the size of it?

WINCHELL: What are you muttering about?

MARTIN: What can I do for you, sir?

WINCHELL: *What can I do for you, sir?* You can stand here and over-see while I go over my take-away. Maybe you think I was born yesterday.

MARTIN: *(Aside.)* Try a hundred years ago.

WINCHELL: Your irritating habit of muttering has effected your tip, I hope you understand that.

MARTIN: No, really?

WINCHELL: A-ha! I knew it! I sent three shrimp pieces to be wrapped up and there are only two here.

MARTIN: I took care of your wrap-up myself *(Aside.)* just to prevent something like this *(Back to WINCHELL.)* and you sent two shrimps to be wr—

WINCHELL: I sent *three* shrimp pieces to be wrapped. It must be the end of your shift. A little hungry? *(Aside.)* It's profitable to check these things, I probably would have had a hundred pounds of food pilfered by peckish waiters over the years if I weren't so vigilant. *(Back to MARTIN.)* Did you enjoy it?

MARTIN: You're saying I ate *food* off your *plate*? That I ate food off your plate? *(Aside.)* Shit—I'm going to lose it. *(Back to WINCHELL.)* I don't want your stinking shrimp! They feed us here! I've never taken food off a customer's plate! I've never even thought of it! That's disgusting and dirty and—

WINCHELL: I'm the *customer*. If you want my business again, you'll give me another shrimp piece to take home and maybe I'll forget this.

MARTIN: I'll be damned if I give you a shrimp, you liar.

WINCHELL: Did you hear that everybody? This waiter just called me a liar! Where's my dinner plate? The menu says I get eight shrimp pieces. Let's count the shrimp shells to prove it. It's a science called *forensics*.

MARTIN: You bloody know it's in the garbage can by now.

WINCHELL: Then the onus is on you, the last man with the shrimps! Your boss is looking. Oh-oh, you're in trouble. Don't you think you'd better get me an additional shrimp piece?

> *MARTIN trembles with rage. WINCHELL begins writing in his little black book. MIA, returning from powder room, hurries over.*

MIA: What's wrong? I thought I heard—

WINCHELL: Mia, the waiter stole a shrimp.

MIA: *The waiter stole a shrimp.* OK, let's wind this little celebration up. Here's your spaghetti. Ten strings I believe? And two shrimp, the basket of bread rolls, the butter, of course the sugar packets. I'm very sorry, young man.

WINCHELL: You're siding with him? I have a missing shrimp!

MIA: Very, very sorry. *(Aside.)* Sorry I'm twice his age. *(To MARTIN.)* I'm sorry.

MARTIN: I'm sorry for you.

WINCHELL: How dare you be sorry for my wife.

MIA: And it's our anniversary.

MARTIN: Harsh.

WINCHELL: Would you care to step outside, you imperti-
             nent—

MIA: Winchell, if you don't walk away this second, I'm
             going to throw your takeout on the floor.

WINCHELL: She'll do it, too. Now who are you sorry for?

             WINCHELL and MIA go to leave but —

MIA: Just a second, did you tip him?

WINCHELL: Of course I—

             *MIA and WINCHELL lunge for the bill folder in
             MARTIN's hand. They struggle. MIA wins and
             opens it.*

MIA: Pull out your wallet, you liar.

             WINCHELL reluctantly takes out his coin purse.

WAITER: I wouldn't take your coins if you—

WINCHELL: He says he doesn't want a tip.

MIA: Not your coin purse, your wallet!

WINCHELL: But he stole a shrimp!

MIA: I give up. Out!

             MIA and WINCHELL exit restaurant.

             Oh my god, I left my favourite lipstick in the
             bathroom, I can't believe I have to show my face in
             there again.

MIA hurries back in.

WINCHELL: *(Calling after her.)* I hope no one's taken it—it's not fun to be robbed! *(Aside.)* That's a wife for you. No support, no sympathy, in conclusion, completely useless.

WINCHELL begins erasing from his little black book. MIA comes out, shows him the lipstick, and walks off. WINCHELL follows.

Scene 2

EMILY, trying to help with the ironing, hollers for RICHARD. He enters, aghast.

RICHARD: My god don't touch that with an iron! Put it down, slowly! That's an actual Coco Channel suit. Never, never an iron! You *steam.*

EMILY: I hate this stodgy thing.

RICHARD: Look at these seams, you moron!

EMILY: You think I'm an idiot!

RICHARD: I was kidding. But leave the ironing to me.

EMILY: It's not funny. I was born with looks that make men dizzy.

RICHARD: I know.

EMILY: And beautiful people are treated a certain way because they're beautiful.

RICHARD: True.

EMILY: And that's wrong. But not in my case. I'm a fool.

RICHARD: Don't talk that way about my best friend!

EMILY: I've got tons of issues you'd never dream of to look

at me. I'm insecure about my intelligences. Teachers were always taking out their rotten lives on me. Oh, I've got tons of issues you'd never dream of to look at me. I've never had a real friend before you. All the girls hated me because I was too pretty. No, I had a friend named Karen Stuart, we were equally as pretty for quite awhile. But when we came back after summer in grade 7…no more Karen. She got fat.

RICHARD: I'm sure you had plenty of boyfriends.

EMILY: 'Boys'. Exactly. You get them, but who wants them? As soon as I had my orgasm, I asked them to take me home. I hurt so many guys. Now God is punishing me for my former ways. I'm completely clueless about life and love, Richard. I'm in way over my head.

RICHARD: Well keeping your engagement a secret must be stressf—

EMILY: I know, shut up, don't you think I know? But we have to put it over just right with the folks. Oh my god, I'm in love. Martin's a man. I mean, a man. Martin…oh my god.

RICHARD: Yes, he's… *(RICHARD coughs to get out of finishing.)*

EMILY: I know, right? I want to be a different kind of woman for Martin so I can keep him, more substantial, someone who has a cause, who's really, really deep. Do you think Martin wants me for my family's money?

RICHARD: Nooo, he—

EMILY: Whatever, I'm so pathetically in love with him, I don't even care—so long as he's mine. I've got a confession to make. Martin is set on our wedding taking place in St. Bart's. And I said daddy'd pay.

RICHARD: You what?

EMILY: Everybody thinks I'm rich because of my parent's business and this house *(Aside.)* and because I don't do anything *(Back to RICHARD.)* but I'm basically a slave here without a dime. But I can't tell Martin that! What if his love can be bought for a price and I can't pay? I think I'd die. I want him. I want to own him! I've never been dumped—did you know that?

RICHARD: No—but I believe it. You're gorgeous.

EMILY: Thank you. Do you think Martin notices? He never says anything about how pretty I am!

RICHARD: He's not blind.

EMILY: True. Ugh.

RICHARD: What?!

EMILY: There's something I've been meaning to ask you…

RICHARD: Anything!

EMILY: This is totes inappropes.

RICHARD: What?

EMILY: He said we can never do the same position twice.

RICHARD: Really? *(Aside.)* Really?

EMILY: Like, never. And there's only 64 positions in the Kama Sutra but he says they don't know anything.

RICHARD: Uh…

EMILY: I kind of wondered if he was…maybe bored already. Sometimes I just want to lie there, you know, but apparently we can't. Lying there was enough for all the other guys I was with. Not to make it sound like I always was just lying there.

RICHARD: Of course not!

EMILY: Do you think he's bored with me?

RICHARD: I think he's fascinated with you.

EMILY: OK, good. 'Cause he just kind of sits there sometimes. He just looks out the window. And I study his face. He's got a few wrinkles. I sit and look at his wrinkles and wonder what gave him that wrinkle, and what gave him that wrinkle, you know? What would he want with me? He's got these wrinkles of experience. I have nothing. I'm a blank.

RICHARD: If I were to commit the crime of generalization—I think that's the way men like it.

EMILY: See how insecure I am? I'm afraid of putting myself in his hands—but I yearn to. I long for marriage, I dread marriage. I'm confused! *(Aside.)* I'm confused.

RICHARD: Only idiots aren't afraid of marriage.

EMILY: You think marriage is dumb?

RICHARD: For some, for some. But there's something enticing about the idea all the same. And I mean, the wedding dress!

EMILY: I found one.

RICHARD: Excuse me?

EMILY: I'm sorry—Martin insisted we shop for it.

RICHARD: *(Aside.)* Oh he did, did he?

EMILY: At times it seemed to be more about him trying on Armani suits than me picking a dress.

RICHARD: *(Aside.)* No. *(To EMILY.)* Really?

EMILY: But I *found* it! A princess ball gown. Doesn't every girl deserve to be a princess on her day? *(Aside.)* I do!

RICHARD: *(Aside.)* I do.

EMILY: I knew the dress was mine because I cried when I saw myself in it. And do you know what? Martin cried too! He cried and cried, but he was laughing at the same time. I'd never seen him cry before.

RICHARD: *(Aside.)* I would have loved to have seen that. *(Back to EMILY.)* Did you put a downpayment on it?

EMILY: My education fund from Grandma.

RICHARD: I didn't know you had an education fund from Grandma.

EMILY: Had. But it's *my* inheritance. You can't tell me how to spend it from beyond the grave.

RICHARD: If I don't like the dress…

EMILY: You'll love it!

RICHARD: I'm so disappointed I can't speak. Which bridal salon—Olivia Couture?

EMILY: Yes.

RICHARD: Traitor.

EMILY: Don't make me feel worse than I do!

RICHARD: I really don't want to harp, but saying yes to the dress without me is giving me a signal. Maybe we're not as close as I thought.

EMILY: I wanted you there so badly, but it was Martin, honestly, he kept nagging! I love you and I know you love me. Don't you show it every day?

RICHARD: Can I ever forget the way you risked your life, snatching me from the fury of the waves when I hit my head windsurfing, how you dragged me back to shore, the rasp in your lungs toward the end there. I was terrified I'd drag you down, you're so tiny, you used every ounce of strength you had.

EMILY: I'm a strong swimmer—I've yet to meet the man I couldn't pull in. I wish I still felt that confident on shore.

RICHARD: You saved my life—I save yours.

EMILY: Have you gone any way to gaining my father's confidence?

RICHARD: I'm making progress.

EMILY: It's progress that he hired you and he's paying you.

RICHARD: I'm still here on a trial basis.

EMILY: But the two week free trial ended yesterday!

RICHARD: He told me yesterday he needed another two weeks to know for sure.

EMILY: That dirty old miser!

RICHARD: I belly crawled to get into service, do you think two more weeks is going to kill me? I ingratiate myself constantly to gain favour. What I like to do the most is pretend to agree with him. I applaud whatever he does—and I never have to worry about overdoing it.

EMILY: Poor Daddy.

RICHARD: Poor Daddy nothing. I'm winning his trust, compliment by compliment. With trust comes influence. He's a slow basting turkey and we're going to pick his bones clean.

EMILY: You keep saying that—but how will we get our hands on some money?

RICHARD: We have to—

RICHARD
and EMILY: Play it by ear.

EMILY: That sounds so time consuming. *I want money.* Oh, FML, I should just elope and start from nothing—if Martin'll have me poor. There's no shame in it.

RICHARD: Martin? Satisfied being poor? Yes, there's shame in being poor. So much shame! And if you really didn't mind either way, you wouldn't be mooning about St. Bart's and your princess ball gown. You're waiting for the money, girl.

EMILY: I could teach swimming but I hate kids. I could teach yoga but it'd fuck with my zen.

RICHARD: You don't want to do that.

EMILY: My mother has some money of her own. I could probably get some. But daddy's got half the cafés.

RICHARD: Your father the miser is going to pay.

Offstage sounds of an argument.

MIA: *(Offstage.)* My complete and utter humiliation—

WINCHELL: *(Offstage.)* How do you carry on a constant monlogue without breathing?

MIA: *(Offstage.)* —every time we are out in public—

EMILY: Oh, no, that's them—and they're arguing again. The dinner mustn't have gone well.

RICHARD: Big surprise! Let's spy!

EMILY: No, I want to talk to them! Just act nomal.

MIA and WINCHELL entering.

MIA: You never change. Never!

WINCHELL: You just love the sound of your own voice.

RICHARD: May I take your bag, madame?

MIA: No you may not. I've seen you mooning over my things. You're liable to really take it.

RICHARD: Madame! How could you—?! Never!

WINCHELL: A fresh pencil, Richard.

RICHARD provides from his breast pocket.

RICHARD: Here you are, sir.

WINCHELL: That will be all, Richard.

RICHARD: Madame, I—

MIA: Oh, off you go.

RICHARD exits.

MIA: Are you actually paying him yet?

WINCHELL: I felt it necessary to extend his probation.

MIA: No.

EMILY: Mommy and Daddy, how was your anniversary dinner? Huh?

MIA: Lovely, thank you, darling.

EMILY: Daddy, did you like it?

WINCHELL: The prices were outrageous.

EMILY: But you weren't paying, daddy.

WINCHELL: It still spoils things. That and the wondering about where you got the money to buy said gift certificate.

You wouldn't happen to be siphoning cash off your education fund now would—

EMILY: Mommy! Daddy's nagging about the education fund again!

MIA: Winchell, we're not doing this again!

WINCHELL: I've told you it's a mistake to allow her access to her educa—

MIA: It was in my mother's will Emily have her own account for her education fund and the topic is *closed*. If we don't have trust amongst ourselves, what do we have?

WINCHELL: Then where did you get the money, Emily?

EMILY: Boo! I led a yoga class when one of the teachers got a flat, are you satisfied?

MIA: Good girl!

WINCHELL: Any chance of getting on there full time?

EMILY: No. Can we get back to your dinner? How was the service?

WINCHELL: Terrible.

MIA: Grrrr. Why don't you just thank your beautiful daughter for the gift certificate and leave it.

WINCHELL: Why don't you go pour yourself another glass of wine.

MIA: Best idea I've heard all day. No, my whole life. Let me amend that: my whole married life.

            MIA exits.

WINCHELL: Richard!

            RICHARD enters.

RICHARD: Sir?

WINCHELL: She's headed for the pinot, Richard.

> *RICHARD bolts out after MIA.*

EMILY: What was wrong with the service?

WINCHELL: Oh, Emily, could I get your Jane Henry on this?

EMILY: What is it?

WINCHELL: Just something for the business. Need a witness.

EMILY: *(Signing.)* What was wrong with the service?

WINCHELL: The waiter stole a shrimp from my take-away. I'm going to call the restaurant in the morning and demand restitution.

EMILY: Oh, Daddy, don't, please, you know you always get mad about your take-away, please just leave it this once—

> *MIA re-enters drinking a glass of wine, followed by RICHARD with a watering can who pretends to water plants. WINCHELL sees her and tries to slip the paper EMILY has signed back into his blazer pocket.*

MIA: What's the paper?

WINCHELL: Nothing.

EMILY: I witnessed something for the business.

MIA: You—? Let me see that.

WINCHELL: No, it's dealt with.

MIA: Give me that.

> *MIA puts down her wine and she and WINCHELL wrestle for the paper, MIA wins and reads.*

*RICHARD discreetly tops up MIA's wine glass
with water from the can.*

Emily, you've just signed a lease to rent your room
here for $850 per month.

*MIA picks up her wine. She is confused the glass is
full but swigs anyway.*

EMILY: Huh?

MIA: You had that all typed up and in your pocket ready
              to go.

WINCHELL: That's a modest rent for a large room with an en
              suite in the Gates, given Winnipeg's rental market.
              And she eats all our food.

EMILY: Can someone please explain WTF?

MIA: Leave mommy and daddy alone, please, Emily.

              *WINCHELL is writing in his little black book.
              EMILY exits.*

Winch, I've appreciated the fact we could always
pay our bills. There were flowers in the house, even
if they were out of our garden.

*MIA sets her glass down. When the moment is right,
RICHARD tops it with water.*

Every nickel spent above bread and water has
been a battle. I had my special money to draw on,
thank god, and I've had my friends, my activities,
my girl... Excuse me, am I keeping you? Your little
notebook. Explain it to me, if you don't mind.

WINCHELL: It took some time but you're finally taking an
              interest.

MIA: I've always been interested Winchell, I just didn't
              know if I could stand the excitement.

WINCHELL: Now we've retired, I've not ceased to have a daily cash intake! You've heard of the hundred mile diet? This is my hundred dollar plan. Every day, I find a way, come hell or high water, to make one hundred dollars. I record the money I make and the way I make it in this ledger. And I can tell you, it's not always easy—but I sleep better at night when I've made my hundred!

MIA: But how in the world were you clever enough to make money during supper?

WINCHELL: Well…you know.

MIA: I think I do know Winch, but why don't you to tell me. You weren't spending anything. Everything was paid for by a gift certificate from our beautiful daughter—

WINCHELL: And what do you suppose the catch is?

MIA: It was a lovely gesture for our anniversary, you paranoid old— But what were the notations you were taking?

WINCHELL: It's not always cash money I make, but money in kind.

MIA: Yes, of course—go on.

WINCHELL: So in effect, if I, say, walk instead of take the bus, I've "made" the bus fare, I notate that, and that's part of my grand total for the day.

MIA: Why in hell do you own that gorgeous car when you insist on taking the bus?

MIA picks up her wine glass.

WINCHELL: I'll take the car the day I can afford the gas!

MIA: And so if you start an argument with a waiter over nothing and use that as an excuse not to tip him, you've "made", what, forty dollars?

WINCHELL: Forty-two, if we tipped him 20% on the bill we would have had if we didn't have the gift certificate! And I've just made my daily quota!

MIA: You've never tipped 20% in your life.

WINCHELL: Touché.

MIA: He was a nice young man, that waiter. He's probably using his tips to put himself through college.

WINCHELL: He gets an hourly wage, why should I supplement it?

MIA: You picked a fake fight with him over a non-existent shrimp after you wheedled and begged for a larger slice of cake and he gave it to you! The extra bit of cake probably had a value in kind, too—

WINCHELL: Only fifty cents.

             MIA takes a swig and it tastes weird. She looks around and seeing RICHARD in the corner with his can, chases him offstage with:

MIA: Out! Out, you nuisance! (*Back to WINCHELL.*) You misanthropic tightwad, you close-fisted creep. You robbed him!

WINCHELL: What did you say? Richard! Robbers!

             RICHARD runs back in, on alert to protect, with a rolling pin.

WINCHELL: Robbers, Richard!

MIA: I didn't say there were robbers, I said you robbed that boy.

WINCHELL: Oh, thank god. You may go, Richard.

             RICHARD, also relieved, exits.

MIA: If you cared so much about robbers, you wouldn't let a strange man, who limps in off the street and begs to be your butler—

WINCHELL: But I've got him buttling for free.

MIA: Yes, yes, yes, he's buttling for free. You don't find that suspicious in any way?

WINCHELL: I'm not so naive as you think! I'm watching him at all times.

MIA: At all times. Right. So you'll let this stranger in— and then turn around and try to rob your daughter.

WINCHELL: She's not doing any buttling!

MIA: A lease for $850? That I cannot forgive.

WINCHELL: I'll go down to $750.

> *WINCHELL takes a fresh lease out of his pocket.*

MIA: You have a lease for $750 prepared as well?

> *WINCHELL grins awkwardly.*

You are a miser, Winchell. You are a sick man, a miser, you are a miserly man with a miserly spirit.

WINCHELL: To whom are you referring?

MIA: Misers. Stingy old scoundrels.

WINCHELL: Where? You mean those ones in B.C.? Shhhh!

MIA: What are you talking about, B.C.?

WINCHELL: Quit shouting the word 'miser' by the window, it implies cash sewn into mattress!

MIA: You've gone off the deep end.

WINCHELL: You may as well rent a billboard with a picture of yourself swathed in haute couture, announcing we have money!

MIA: I buy my clothes with my special money.

WINCHELL: The robbers don't know that!

MIA: *(Shouting.)* Miser! Miser! Miser!

WINCHELL: Are you trying to murder me!? Robbers'll come and
              cut my throat!

MIA: Well, how the deuce—?! Is it likely you'll be robbed
              when you keep all your best things under lock and
              key in your study and stand guard day and night?
              Just what do you have in there?

WINCHELL: It's my money, I'll do as I please.

MIA: Your money is our money, so please you. Do you
              have cash in there?

WINCHELL: No, I do not have cash in there. But let's talk about
              the cash in your bobble account.

MIA: Richard! Robbers!

              RICHARD enters.

RICHARD: Madame?

MIA: Make yourself useful—get the pinot grigio.

              RICHARD leaves slowly, listening.

WINCHELL: I'll say it again: I demand your bobble account to be
              made a joint account.

MIA: You've been harping on this since we retired.

WINCHELL: Why should you share my toothpick money and
              the café money and I shouldn't get some of your
              bobble money?

MIA: It's like a brain fever.

WINCHELL: If you made your bobble account a joint one and let me manage your monies, I'd double your investment in a year, you know I would.

MIA: But what would you charge for the service?

WINCHELL: It's not fair!

MIA: Who does fair anymore?

WINCHELL: I'm palpitating!

MIA: Winchell, my money is my money, but your money is our money. Accept it. There's nothing you can do about it.

WINCHELL: I know. And the lawyer charged me a two hundred dollar consultation fee just to tell me that! Oops.

MIA: You consulted a lawyer?

WINCHELL: Yes…

MIA: That makes it final. I'm divorcing you, Winch.

WINCHELL: This isn't entirely unexpected. But you'll still be happily married to your bobble account.

RICHARD enters with the wine.

MIA: Fill 'er up.

WINCHELL: I've found out something quite illuminating. We don't need lawyers. We can file the papers ourselves for a small fee.

WINCHELL takes the divorce papers out of his breast pocket.

MIA: These are…filled out. But they're only good if the divorce is uncontested.

WINCHELL: Obviously! But we all know the worst thing about divorce is the lawyers panting for their fees like a dog for a bone!

MIA: You're as cold as your coins.

WINCHELL: Not at all. With your precious bobble money, you'll want for nothing. And we'll split our assets…down the middle.

MIA: Hard to choke that one out, eh? You've certainly thought this through.

WINCHELL: This divorce will save me a considerable yearly sum. But even with Emily paying rent…she saps the utilities to the breaking point and eats like a hog. The pressure will really be off if she moves out. She certainly has enough boyfriends to choose from, I hope one will take her off my hands.

MIA: Winch, you're going to need a lawyer, and a good one. I spent the better part of my life having you dole out the pennies.

WINCHELL: Dole out the—look at this mansion! This house isn't good enough for you?

MIA: You tried to buy a duplex in Point Douglas. And I did all the upgrades with my money! Stainless steel appliances, granite countertops—all my money. And these Eames chairs—

WINCHELL: Just a second—

MIA: Left to me by my mother—

WINCHELL: Left to us—

MIA: My mother—

WINCHELL: Left to us. You take two, I take two—

MIA: Or how about I take all four. Winchell, I intend to take you to the cleaners. If only for the joy of seeing you spend.

WINCHELL: OK, fine, I'll pay you back for half of the upgrades to avoid squabbling. But I told you at the time! There was no reason you had to go high end!

MIA: Oh, you'll pay me half now, will you?

WINCHELL: Come, let's have one of those amicable splits like they do in the European movies you love so much. You don't need to exact revenge for the upgrades.

MIA: Wait till I exact revenge for that $850 lease.

WINCHELL: You've already dickered me down to $750!

MIA: I just keep thinking how upset you made that waiter.

WINCHELL: You're going to—

MIA: —take you to the cleaners.

WINCHELL: Why—because I didn't tip the waiter?

MIA: I like the sound of that:yes. Because you didn't tip the waiter.

WINCHELL: Your conscience will not allow this!

MIA: You'll find me at Hotel Fort Garry.

MIA exits.

WINCHELL: Richard!

RICHARD enters.

RICHARD: Sir?

WINCHELL: Out of the blue, my wife has threatened to sue me for divorce and she's sworn to take me for everything I'm worth. Not that I have much! Just a very modest savings scraped together, after a life of work, and raising a spoilt child with all those attendant costs, and a socialite wife who drapes herself in the most extravagant fashions season after season. After all that sucking of my marrow for forty years, she intends to get her claws on what I do have, like a vulture picking over bare bones.

RICHARD: Sir, I'm honoured you've chosen to confide in me.

WINCHELL: I want your advice before I call another lawyer. Their consultation fees are stratospheric! You effeminate men, you understand male/female unions much clearer than the rest of us.

RICHARD: I am your very humble servant.

WINCHELL: Is there hope? Give me hope!

RICHARD: Hope? Why, sir. You'll miss her.

WINCHELL: Miss her? Hope—hope to beat her in court!

RICHARD: There is always hope. You know women. This may just be a bid for attention.

WINCHELL: Well, she's got it.

RICHARD: What would you say binds you two together most powerfully?

WINCHELL: Binds us?

RICHARD: Think.

WINCHELL: Well….in our early years, it was business. When I met her she was a waitress. I had just invented the menthol flavoured toothpick. But I was still in my salad days, wearing holes in my shoes pedalling toothpicks from restaurant to restaurant.

RICHARD: (Pointing at WINCHELL's amazingly patched shoes.) Not those shoes?!

WINCHELL: The very same. She was entranced by me and my entrepreneurial spirit. And for me, she was a revelation. I'd never met a woman who was so focused on money. We'd drink black coffee and eat ham sandwiches and talk about getting money. Then she came up with the idea of the bobble-headed figure.

RICHARD: The what?

WINCHELL: You know, the figures with the heads that wiggle-wobble in the back window of car.

RICHARD: That was her idea?

WINCHELL: Mia was the first to think to patent the bobble-heads. I'll never forget the moment she came up with the idea, she was glowing with a religious light. My wife is what's known as a patent troll. That patent, and a few others, bring her a modest income. And even though I helped her with her research, and the finagling, she was clever enough to get the patents solely in her name. She just slipped that by me with a smile, and I, so dazzled... We wanted success and the finer things in life, and mostly, we wanted other people's money. There is a particular joy in accumulating a large sum of money through a lot of tiny transactions. It's like slipping the spare change out of the world's pants pocket when they've gone to bed. We wed. Now this was a long time ago, but Mia and I felt that one day, in the right setting, with the right coffee, people would pay as much as ten dollars for a good, big slice of cake. Cake was cheap back then. But we held on, struggling side by side, until we were able to charge a ridiculous mark-up on cakes. She had invested the capital for the first café from her bobble head money...and used her old family cake recipes—oh, no! I'd forgotten all this! It gets worse and worse! You're not helping at all!

RICHARD: Keep going—there may be something in our favour.

WINCHELL: My heart is pounding. Midway through our marriage, everything clicked. Our cafés became established. It was all modest, mind you! But somewhat secure. I can't say we became happy, though I don't remember why. She became sour and argumentative. She didn't understand that success doesn't mean you suddenly become freewheeling! I fought constantly to keep us on track.

RICHARD: What else? Think more personal.

WINCHELL: She'd given up the idea of children long before, but suddenly she found herself pregnant in her autumn years, and there was joy again, for a time.

RICHARD: She must have had Emily in her forties. That's not her autumn years.

WINCHELL: Well, whatever you call it, then.

RICHARD: It's regarded as the prime of life, I think.

WINCHELL: I'm sure you know best. Back to the story. Suddenly she was pregnant.

RICHARD: Oh.

WINCHELL: Oh what?

RICHARD: Go on.

WINCHELL: Anyway, she had the child, we raised the child. And here we are. She's harvested my fields for forty years and now she'll leave them barren.

RICHARD: Forgive my intrusion. You're a highly attractive man. Irresistible, no doubt. Your physical relationship? It sustained a long marriage.

WINCHELL: I've never had any complaints. But this woman— she'll be the first to admit very little satisfies her. But women are self-sustaining, yes? Happy as anything with their vibrating devices.

RICHARD: OK. Establishing your business brought you together the first half of your marriage, and your

child and your business kept you together the last
half. No physical relationship.

WINCHELL: Marriage is like buying a car. As soon as you stick
your key in the ignition, the value goes down, and
they cost you and cost you. You've clarified the
works, Richard. I can think of nothing that would
sway a judge to my side. I must win her back.

RICHARD: Eh?

WINCHELL: Why do you say 'Eh' like that?

RICHARD: You're going to win her back?

WINCHELL: It's hopeless to fight her in divorce court.

RICHARD: But...how?

WINCHELL: Come on, man, I'm relying on you! You'll know
what it'll take to woo my wife again.

RICHARD: *(Aside.)* Again?

WINCHELL: You will figure out what I should do.

RICHARD: Yes—of course I will! But...you don't seem to like
her and she doesn't seem to like you, her own bad
taste of course, there's no accounting for it...

WINCHELL: Yes, but she'll fleece me in court. How do I keep
her?

RICHARD: Well...you...you... But the old fireworks don't fire
like they once did—

WINCHELL: But she'll fleece me, Richard, she'll fleece me.

RICHARD: True. She'll fleece you. There's no countering that.

WINCHELL: What do we do, man?

RICHARD: We win her back!

WINCHELL looks offstage.

WINCHELL: Did you hear the dog bark?

RICHARD: I've never heard the dog bark.

WINCHELL: That's a good thing. He is a guard dog. That would mean trouble.

RICHARD: He seems far too weak and hungry to do anything but lie in the yard.

WINCHELL: If all I did was lie in the yard guarding, I wouldn't need much to eat, either. But perhaps Mia's trying to unlock the garage and get my car. She's always coveted it. I've siphoned the gas out of the tank and sealed it in Tupperware so it doesn't evaporate, but I wouldn't miss the look on her face when I catch her for the world. Richard, get my daughter to sign this lease, please.

RICHARD: Sir?

> *WINCHELL hands RICHARD the new lease and goes, EMILY enters.*

EMILY: You're not going to help him win my mother back after what he said about sticking the key in the ignition!

RICHARD: We can't rub him the wrong way.

EMILY: I'm not signing that lease.

RICHARD: I think you should.

EMILY: Who's side are you on?

RICHARD: I'm here for one reason—you. Sign the lease.

EMILY: But if my mother sues him for divorce and wins, I'll definitely get her to give me a big wedding and some money.

RICHARD: Do you realize how long these things can take? There's something you need to know. Your dad's been filtering all kinds of cash out of the cafés, and keeping it somewhere on the premises, to get it out of your mother's hands.

EMILY: When were you planning on telling me this?

RICHARD: I've seen him twice through the keyhole of his study ironing bills beside a strongbox.

EMILY: Ironing bills?

RICHARD mimes ironing.

RICHARD: What we have to do is find that box—fast. You'll get money out of your mother—and a fat cash dowry that Daddy won't dare report missing. It will set you up for life.

EMILY: You think it's that much?

RICHARD: I do.

EMILY: Money! Money! I'm going to get money! Whoa—I'm gonna to rob my dad.

RICHARD: And he robbed your mom. And they both charge ten dollars for a slice of cake. Is that any less criminal?

EMILY: OK, you're right. YOLO. Money sitting in a box is just a waste. I'll use the money. That's not a waste. It just makes sense. Logic. Like that dude on *Star Trek*. What's a little friendly robbing? The box has got to be in his study. He lives in there like a hermit, and when he's not inside, he's checking the lock.

RICHARD: But he has the key on him at all times.

EMILY: He's ridic about his keys. We're screwed.

RICHARD: But maybe it's buried in the garden.

EMILY: Why would you think that?

RICHARD: Earth under his fingernails.

EMILY: OK, you pick the locks. All you need is a pokey thing. I saw it on TV. I'll dig up the garden—

RICHARD: We can't run around willy nilly. Keep calm and get him in a good humour, so he'll let his guard down and expose the hiding place. Sign the lease.

            EMILY signing.

EMILY: Whatever with this lease. I could marry Martin in St. Bart's by sundown tomorrow if we find it.

RICHARD: Has your dress been altered?

EMILY: I only ordered it on the weekend. My first fitting's in four months.

RICHARD: Call them and tell them you want it now.

EMILY: You can't do that with a wedding dress.

RICHARD: You can when you're rich. No begging, no pleading, just tell them. Never mind, leave it to me.

            WINCHELL enters.

WINCHELL: What are you two talking about? Leave what to you?

RICHARD: Forgive me, sir, for letting my feelings run away with me and talking to your daughter this way, but she was intending to ask you for some allowance, and I strongly felt she should go and get a job and bring in some money! But it's not my place. I beg your—

WINCHELL: No, no, I give you a free hand! I invest Richard with a full parental authority over you. Emily, you must do exactly as he tells you.

EMILY: If you say so. *(EMILY begins to leave.)* Oh by the way, nice one, daddy, tricking me into signing a lease.

Here's the new one. I signed it. *(EMILY shows him then rips it up and it drops to the floor.)* Whoops.

WINCHELL: Your mother has agreed we drop the rent a whole $100 to $750. I think you'll agree it's quite a good haggle down.

EMILY: That's awesome—when I don't have any money.

WINCHELL: There's a little thing we did in the olden days called Getting A Job.

EMILY: Cute, daddy. What if I don't need to rent your lousy room?

WINCHELL: Can I help you pack?

EMILY: What would you charge for that help?

WINCHELL: Nothing. Because there's a legal term called 'squatter' that now applies to you, and I would hate to see my little girl go to jail.

EMILY: You're so sweet, maybe I'll give you a big surprise one day.

WINCHELL: As long as it doesn't cost me.

EMILY: A big, fat surprise, daddy-o…

RICHARD: I'm sorry, sir.

WINCHELL: Not your fault, Richard, she gets it from her mother.

RICHARD referring to the ripped lease.

RICHARD: I'm not going to clean this up.

EMILY: I'm not the butler.

RICHARD: You need to learn a thing or two.

WINCHELL: I'd be grateful if you could teach her anything.

EMILY: Bite it, daddy.

RICHARD: Sir, it is I who is grateful to you.

WINCHELL: You need to learn, Emily.

RICHARD: I couldn't agree with you more, sir.

WINCHELL: The self-respect that comes from honest work.

RICHARD: The dignity of service.

WINCHELL: Well put, Richard.

RICHARD: Thank you, sir.

EMILY: Want me to leave you two alone?

RICHARD: I need to have a very serious word with you in the garden, Emily.

WINCHELL: And I'd like a word—about the things we discussed, Richard.

EMILY: What things?

WINCHELL: Man talk, my dear.

RICHARD: Pick up that paper.

                    EMILY does so grudgingly.

WINCHELL: That's more than I've seen her do since birth.

EMILY: I'm going to rupture myself laughing, Daddy.

RICHARD: Pleasing personal grooming would be something you could start on anytime, sir. You know, neatening up, regard to body odours.

WINCHELL: It's in the details, eh?

RICHARD: Oh, very much so.

WINCHELL: Fascinating.

RICHARD: Now, Emily, learn: that goes in the recycling bin— or you can mulch it for the garden. Another lesson:

money is the most precious thing in the world, young lady. You ought to thank heaven that you have such a good father.

WINCHELL: Oh, Richard.

RICHARD: Sir?

WINCHELL: This is looking very good for you and your probationary state.

RICHARD: Thank-you, sir. *(Exiting with EMILY.)* Your father knows the value of things. Money counts more than good looks, youth, birth, honour, wisdom…

RICHARD and EMILY exit.

WINCHELL: *(To audience.)* How lucky I am this man came to my door. Do I trust his motives? No. But nor do I trust anyone else's! And it's as if I've hired her a private tutor. They're not cheap.

WINCHELL notates in his little black book as he goes into his office. MIA comes through pulling a suitcase on wheels. Hearing the sound of digging from the garden, MIA looks through the window.

MIA: Emily, come in for moment.

EMILY enters, muddy.

What are you doing out there?

EMILY: Planting a vegetable patch.

MIA: I need to talk to you. I know you're all grown up now but these things can still be difficult. Baby, your father and I are separating.

EMILY: No one else could put up with him. What would happen to Daddy without you around?

MIA: We'll see. Give me a hug— You're filthy. Later!

EMILY: Mom, I have to tell you something important, too.

MIA: Yes, my beauty?

EMILY: I'm engaged.

MIA: What?! To whom?

EMILY: That guy I mentioned to you, Martin.

MIA: That boy you met last month surfing? Oh my god, Emily, can you learn nothing from what I'm going through? Love him, love him to death, but for god's sake, you don't have to marry him!

EMILY: But I want to be with him forever.

MIA: Honey, marriage isn't an inextricable bond. Gather all your beach bum friends in the back garden, light some candles, vow your love forever and drink a case of wine. I'll be there cheering you on. And I'll really be cheering when you get sick of each other's faces two years down the road and can walk away with no strings.

EMILY: But Mommy, there's more.

MIA: Here it comes.

EMILY: He wants the wedding in St. Bart's.

              MIA sputters.

              It was all him—I'd never heard of St. Bart's until he showed me on the internet. It's so pretty, Mommy. And I've put all my education money from grandma down as downpayment on a dress.

MIA: Oh, god. Is that all?

EMILY: They're holding an Armani suit for Martin as well.

MIA: What does he do for a living, pray tell?

EMILY: He works! But it's sporadic.

MIA: Excellent. The sporadic worker. Educated?

EMILY: He's wise.

MIA: *(Aside.)* Beyond his years. *(Back to EMILY.)* How old?

EMILY: Only...fourteen years older.

MIA: I thought you liked boys with freshly scrubbed faces.

EMILY: I did Mommy but Martin's so...so—

MIA: Spare me the details.

EMILY: He wants to protect me.

MIA: From what?

EMILY: He always holds my hand.

MIA: Can't you hold it yourself?

EMILY: We're inseparable.

MIA: Look, you've had the best bang of your young life! Play your cards right and it won't be the last.

EMILY: Mommy!

MIA: You don't have to go through with this!

EMILY: You married Daddy, why can't I marry Martin!?

MIA: Go ahead—marry him, then! But that's not at issue, is it? It's a St. Bart's wedding and designer couture, and who knows what else. Has it ever occurred to you that old man Martin might be a gold digger?

            EMILY weeps.

EMILY: You don't think I can be loved!

MIA: Nonsense, Emily. Oh, my girl, you're going to learn some painful lessons.

EMILY: No, Mommy, I'm not! You might be afraid to take a
              chance now after the way your marriage has turned
              out, but I'm not afraid to love Martin! Let me have
              my chance. It's my turn now! Mom-my!

              *WINCHELL enters, with neatened attire, reeking
              of perfume.*

              Eew, what's that smell?

MIA: God, I'm choking!

WINCHELL: Well, hello, ladies. What's the matter here?

MIA: That smells like my 31 rue Cambon Chanel dumped
              on with a bucket.

WINCHELL: You don't say?

MIA: What's the matter with you, Winchell? You look
              different.

WINCHELL: You noticed.

MIA: Yes, I did.

EMILY: You look kind of dapper, Dad.

WINCHELL: Just a little personal grooming.

EMILY: You almost look handsome.

WINCHELL: How do you like it, Mia my dear?

MIA: Why, I get the feeling that in some pubescent way…
              you're trying to please me, Winchell.

WINCHELL: I want to please you, Mia. Above all else. People can
              change.

MIA: Good. Winch, here's a way for you to please me
              immeasurably. Our daughter is engaged to a wise
              old surfer named Martin. Limber up your cheque
              writing hand. She wants a St. Bart's wedding,

and we're going to give it to her out of our joint account—no arguments. And there'll be a bill for a wedding dress and suit—you'll write the cheque for that as well. We'll pay for those things, Emily, but mind you, not a cent more. I mean it, now. I suppose we should meet him sooner than later. You can reach me at the Hotel Fort Garry.

WINCHELL:· But I thought you might appreciate my new look!

MIA: Oh, I do, Winch.

WINCHELL: Then need you stay at the Hotel Fort Garry?

MIA: It's easy to get married, Emily, but it's hard to stay that way.

EMILY: I have all the invoices right here, Mommy.

MIA: Just give Daddy the total.

EMILY whispers in his ear. WINCHELL is shaken to the core.

Sign the cheque, Winchell. It's easy to get married, Emily, but it's hard to stay that way.

MIA exits.

EMILY: Thank you, Daddy. Daddy, you're palpitating! Oh, good, it's stopped. It's really stopped. Daddy? Daddy, you're not breathing! Daddy? Help, help!

RICHARD: *(Offstage.)* I'm coming!

RICHARD leaps into the room and starts mouth-to-mouth resuscitation.

WINCHELL: Don't bother! Let me go over! My daughter, my only child, my precious flower—remember me. Here, take my wedding ring—give it to your betrothed. You can have it for two hundred dollars.

End of Act I.

Act II

Scene 1

*RICHARD and WINCHELL arrive home,
RICHARD disguised as MIA in the Channel
piece, WINCHELL wearing RICHARD's uniform,
with shades. As they speak, WINCHELL spreads
his arms in an on-the-cross-like fashion, and is
ceremoniously stripped—showing his hospital gown
underneath—down to his boxers and old undershirt
by RICHARD, and dressed in his own clothes which
are waiting neatly folded. RICHARD will achieve a
stunningly fashionable transformation.*

WINCHELL: Are you certain we haven't been followed?

RICHARD: Uhhh… *(Looking outside.)* Yes sir.

WINCHELL: The head nurse was a battle-axe.

RICHARD: I have mixed feelings about the success of our heist,
sir. The doctors and nurses were adamant you were
too sick to go home.

WINCHELL: Sick? They'll really see sick if I get sued for divorce.
I have to keep on top of this situation. You don't
think I look sick, do you?

RICHARD: Sir, you look robust.

WINCHELL: See, what do they know. You've done remarkably
well, Richard, I must say. Disguises—though why
did you need to dress up?

RICHARD: I like to be prepared for anything, sir.

WINCHELL: Fair enough. Your bravery, distracting nurse Ratchett while I made my getaway, your resourcefulness...

RICHARD: Does this mean I've passed my probation?

WINCHELL: Don't get presumptuous. Let's see how you do with this, first. I've made a list of items I'd like your assistance with.

> RICHARD takes the little black book WINCHELL hands him and reads.

RICHARD: 'Win back my wife. Don't let daughter get any more money.' It's good you wrote all this down. Have you considered being honest with Mia?

WINCHELL: I'll save that as a last resort. I'd rather see some of that old Richard Resourcefulness. What plan have you hatched up to help me?

RICHARD: Well...you need to show her you're desirable to other women.

WINCHELL: A bit of the old jealousy, eh?

RICHARD: Don't beg her to take you back, you'll look desperate. Show her you're emotionally strong enough to handle whatever comes your way.

WINCHELL: I see, very good...

RICHARD: That will compound your attractiveness—

WINCHELL: —begun with my personal grooming!

RICHARD: You're catching on!

WINCHELL: What else?

RICHARD: Women want to feel an engagement with their partners—to feel heard. Do you really listen to her?

WINCHELL: Oh, no.

RICHARD: Well, listen to her, connect, pay attention to the little things she says.

WINCHELL: Right.

RICHARD: You always want to...make a woman feel the way she wants to feel.

WINCHELL: What do you mean?

RICHARD: What do all people want to feel?

WINCHELL: I don't know.

RICHARD: What unites rich and poor?

WINCHELL: Having, and not having, money?

RICHARD: Yes, but I think both the tycoon and the lowliest in society need to feel they have some kind of power in the world.

WINCHELL: You're quite a philosopher, Richard.

RICHARD: Give her power. Ask her her opinion—

WINCHELL: Let me write this down.

RICHARD: —and then act on it. Then she will associate you with those positive feelings of power, and she'll in turn want to be with you. Why? So she can feel powerful.

WINCHELL: Ah...yes, yes.

RICHARD: You see?

WINCHELL: I think I do. Give her power.

RICHARD: Yes! So when Mia comes over, what can you do to make her feel powerful?

WINCHELL: I have no idea.

RICHARD: Listen carefully to her, and find ways to give her the power.

WINCHELL: I don't get it.

RICHARD: Let's practice. I'll be Mia, you be you.

WINCHELL: You're Mia?

RICHARD: Yes. Now listen carefully to her. Find ways to give her the power. Hello, Winchell, how've you been?

WINCHELL: Miserable without you, Mia.

RICHARD: No no, don't forget—you don't ever want to appear desperate. You must be strong and attractive, while still giving her the power.

WINCHELL: First it's one way, then it's the other!

RICHARD: Try again. How've you been?

WINCHELL: Bearing up, my dear.

RICHARD: Good. Say something. Ask her how she is.

WINCHELL: I know how she is, she's staying at the Hotel Fort Garry.

RICHARD: Do you want to win her back or don't you?

WINCHELL: More importantly, dear, how are you?

RICHARD: Wonderful—I'm staying at the Hotel Fort Garry.

WINCHELL: Whose side are you on?

RICHARD: I'm playing devil's advocate—work through it.

WINCHELL: I'm glad—you're staying at the Hotel Fort Garry.

RICHARD: I thought you were against my staying there!

WINCHELL: I'm…comforted to know you're comfortable.

RICHARD: Good, sir! Aren't you going to ask me to sit down?

WINCHELL: Sit down, Mia.

RICHARD: Would it be in character for you to have bought her flowers?

WINCHELL: No.

RICHARD: Winchell, it's kind of you to hold this dinner party.

WINCHELL: I didn't have much choice.

RICHARD: Sir...

WINCHELL: It's kind of you to attend.

> *Awkward pause. RICHARD is nodding encouragingly for WINCHELL to proceed with some sort of action.*

Would you care for a beverage?

RICHARD: Very good, sir! Yes, I would like a beverage!

WINCHELL: I know you're partial to the Pinot Grigio.

RICHARD: Good—that shows you notice her preferences! You're giving her power! Please.

WINCHELL: A little too partial if you ask me.

RICHARD: Behave!

> *WINCHELL badly mimes pouring wine and serving it to RICHARD.*

Tasty.

> *Awkward pause.*

Come on, sir, come on.

WINCHELL: Uh... Oh! Your Oxford's hair salon has some sort of wash 'n' blow dry special. I clipped a coupon out of the paper for you.

RICHARD: Did you really, sir?

WINCHELL: Yes, actually!

RICHARD: That is particularly good! Thank you, Winchell. You remembered my salon is Oxford's! I'm touched.

WINCHELL: How can I forget the robbers you shell out good money to for—

RICHARD: No, no, no! Wrong, sir! Godawful! Come on! You're not playing the game! You didn't have to do that! You say something nice, she says thank you, you say you're welcome—and there you leave it!

WINCHELL: Calm down, Richard.

RICHARD: You just leave it! Be gracious! Succinct! Niceness— thank you—you're welcome. Done!

WINCHELL: Alright!

RICHARD: Do it!

WINCHELL: I clipped you a coupon for Oxford's.

RICHARD: Thank you.

WINCHELL: You're welcome.

RICHARD: The end! Again!

WINCHELL: I clipped you a coupon for Oxford's.

RICHARD: Thank you.

WINCHELL: You're welcome.

RICHARD: The end!

WINCHELL: I think I've got it now, Richard.

RICHARD: No you don't! Again—with some semblance of human emotion! Mean it!

WINCHELL: Good lord!

RICHARD: Now!

WINCHELL: I, uh, clipped you a coupon for Oxford's, my dear.

RICHARD: Thank you.

WINCHELL: You're welcome.

RICHARD: In some corners of the world, people show they care with fond touches, a familiar brush of the arm, even a light, friendly kiss. Do you think you can somehow simulate human warmth?

            WINCHELL lightly touches RICHARD's forearm.

WINCHELL: I clipped you a coupon.

            RICHARD moves closer to WINCHELL.

RICHARD: Thank you.

WINCHELL: You're...

            WINCHELL moves in to kiss, but hesitates.

RICHARD: Go on!

WINCHELL: ...welcome.

            WINCHELL and RICHARD kiss. EMILY enters with a yoga ball and begins pilates.

EMILY: Dad? What are you doing here? I thought you were too sick to leave hospital!

WINCHELL: I heard you had a little dinner planned for your mother to meet your inamorato. Did you really dream I'd miss that? Love is not only for the young.

EMILY: OK, YOLO.

WINCHELL: That's what I always say.

EMILY: I thought you were my mother.

RICHARD: Thank you for the compliment.

WINCHELL: Now, everything must work like a Swiss clock tomorrow, so you need to clean up all around, and be careful not to wax the furniture too hard, you'll wear it out. Richard, I'm putting you in charge of the glassware during supper. If anything is broken, it will come out of your potential wages.

RICHARD: Shrewd but fair.

WINCHELL: You're also in charge of the wine but, only serve it when people are thirsty. Don't egg people on to drink. Wait till they have asked several times and always remember to put plenty of water with it. Emily, may I ask what you are doing?

EMILY: Pilates.

RICHARD: Am I to take my apron off, sir?

WINCHELL: Yes, but take care not to spoil your uniform.

RICHARD: Forgive me, sir, but as you know, my charmingly overlarge uniform was given to me with a blotch of oil on the leg, and a tear in the back of my pants, they'll see my—

WINCHELL: See that you keep it against the wall. Face the company at all times and hold a linen napkin casually in front of the stain. Now, you, Emily, are the woman of the household at the moment, and your duty is to keep an eye on what is cleared away from the table and see that nothing is wasted. Bones and greens can go straight into the stock pot.

EMILY: The bones can go to the dog.

WINCHELL: I said the stock pot. I know you like your soup, you eat enough of it. My expectations for tomorrow are very high. We want Mia to have a wonderful time.

EMILY &
RICHARD: Yes, sir.

EMILY: And father…you'll be meeting my fiancé, as well.
                We want him to have a good time, right?

WINCHELL: Obviously we want your latest beach bum—

EMILY: Fiancé.

WINCHELL: —to have a good time. That is the name of the
                game!

EMILY: Thanks.

WINCHELL: You're welcome. Now, last but not least, what to
                serve?

EMILY: Well…

WINCHELL: Here it comes.

EMILY: We'd planned on rack of lamb.

WINCHELL: You planned wrong.

RICHARD: How much money do I have to play with?

WINCHELL: This is what I'm constantly dealing with, people
                wanting to "play with" my money. Money! Money!
                It's the one word everybody knows! Everybody is
                helpless without money. But any cook who knows
                his job can put on a good meal without spending
                much money!

EMILY &
RICHARD: Yes, sir.

WINCHELL: For starters, cook for two. It's an old proverb:
                Provide for two, there's plenty for four.

RICHARD: Very good. So soup, entrée—

WINCHELL: You're not providing for the whole city! Main
                course only!

RICHARD: OK, what about a pork roast?

WINCHELL: Do you know the rate of obesity these days?
             An overloaded table is a death-trap! Give them
             something hearty that will fill them up. Defrost
             that good thick stew with dumplings and chestnuts
             I have in the basement freezer. Something rustic,
             hey? They rediscover these things and call it
             eclectic cuisine.

RICHARD: Very well observed, sir!

WINCHELL: Thank you.

RICHARD: You're welcome.

EMILY: You still have that old stew?

WINCHELL: Emily, give the dog a bath and a brush down and tie
             one of your pretty hair ribbons on his collar—that
             should please your mother.

EMILY: Toby is more like a shadow of a dog than a dog, and
             now you want me to doll him up?

WINCHELL: Well, fine, he's slim, but what does he do?
             Nothing!

EMILY: He's a good, capable dog. Give him a job if it means
             you'll feed him! He'd love to work. He'll pull you
             around on a wheeled cart to save bus fare! You're
             mad or plain cruel not to buy dog food and account
             for every scrap.

WINCHELL: Nonsense. I feed him.

EMILY: Bull! I give half my food to Toby every day, and I've
             done so for years to keep him alive!

WINCHELL: Perhaps you could go get yourself a job at the
             Humane Society and bring in some money!

EMILY: I am the Humane Society in this house! Let me give
             it to you straight—you're a laughingstock! There's

nothing anyone who knows you likes better than to make a running gag of your stinginess. They say you sued your neighbour for theft when his cat chewed a soup bone from your garbage can! I heard you stole oats from a horse's oat bag at a holiday hay ride! There's no going anywhere without you being pulled to pieces. You are a butt and a by-word for everybody and no one ever refers to you except as a miser, a skinflint, and Scrooge!

WINCHELL: I can stop payment on your wedding dress cheque like that!

EMILY: You wouldn't dare cross Mother!

WINCHELL: Your fiancé is a gold-digger! Your engagement is a farce!

EMILY: If you're so against marriage, get a divorce!

EMILY does a war dance of victory.

Get a divorce! Get a divorce!

WINCHELL begins to palpitate.

WINCHELL: Richard, help! She's murdering me!

RICHARD takes her aside and begins to berate her for show but lowers his voice in the process.

RICHARD: Your father is not so unreasonable as you make him out to be! You owe him all the respect under the sky, for the shelter, food and love... What in god's name do you think you're doing?

EMILY: Oh, what?

RICHARD: The plan! The plan!

EMILY: He makes me livid! I can't hold my tongue another second!

RICHARD: The strongbox, you fool!

RICHARD takes WINCHELL aside and speaks loudly to WINCHELL at first, but drops his voice.

Now, look, the girl was carried away. This is classic cold feet. Her fiancé is handsome enough to fall in love with, but a bald head glasses perched on a nose— She know you to be a paragon of manliness. She's acting out because she'll miss you. The first man a girl wants to marry is her father.

WINCHELL: Is that it? You need only have spoken to me, Emily. I am not so unreasonable as all that.

EMILY: My bad, Dad.

WINCHELL: You will always be my own dear girl, rest assured.

EMILY: You can be super sweet sometimes, if only you weren't such a lousy tightwad and—

RICHARD: Look at the nerves of the girl having the boyfriend meet the parents! Off you go, Emily, now, the furniture polish and the shammy are under the—

RICHARD pushes EMILY off.

EMILY: The furniture isn't going to walk away. I'm going to pilates first.

WINCHELL: You've just done pilates, haven't you?

EMILY: That was just a warm-up. Now I'm off to class.

WINCHELL: Let me understand. You pay to roll on a ball in a room with other people rolling on balls.

EMILY: Don't knock it till you try it, old man.

WINCHELL: I'd try it if I could afford— Oh! You know what? I'll drive you to pilates.

RICHARD: Sir?

EMILY: *(Sputters.)* You'll drive me?

WINCHELL: Yes, I'll drive. Richard, can you transfer a half litre of gasoline into my vehicle, please?

RICHARD: Yes, sir.

WINCHELL: I won't be long. This is the key for the gas tank. I'll want these back—immediately.

RICHARD and EMILY can't believe he got the key ring.

EMILY: I'll just grab my mat and towel.

RICHARD backs up to exit.

RICHARD: Certainly, I'll gas you up and get right on with my tasks. And tomorrow, one thing—don't forget to show your vulnerability!

WINCHELL: If I must. And if all else fails—

RICHARD: Honesty.

WINCHELL: I'd rather save that as a last resort. I have a plan of my own.

RICHARD: Oh, sir, I'd say, unequivocally, no plans of your own should come into effect. Your plans probably so far exceed mine in brilliance, they won't mesh.

WINCHELL: My gas— You are being paid.

RICHARD: I am?

WINCHELL: You will be paid if you make it past your probation, but at this rate—oh, Richard, come back, one thing.

RICHARD walks to WINCH who takes the key ring back and slides the office key off.

No one gets my office key, even for a moment. Thought you had the keys to the kingdom, didn't you?

RICHARD: Why no, sir!

WINCHELL: I'm watching you—at all times. Never forget that. My gas, please.

RICHARD: Sir, I—

WINCHELL: My gas, Richard, my gas.

RICHARD: Your gas, sir, indeed, sir. Gas.

> *RICHARD exits, EMILY grabs mat and bag, and she and WINCHELL exit. A sound of a car driving away. RICHARD returns directly and pulls a credit card out of his wallet, and works on the study door lock like a labourer. The door defeats him, and he crumbles to the ground in monumental frustration.*

Scene 2

> *WINCHELL sits in the restaurant of the Hotel Fort Garry in disguise. WAITER (MARTIN) from Act I, Scene 1 approaches.*

MARTIN: Are you ready to make your order?

WINCHELL: I haven't made up my mind yet. I'll have more water and another bread basket.

MARTIN: I apologize, sir, but that's your third bread basket and my manager asked that you make your order.

WINCHELL: I'm not hungry, I'm full on bread.

MARTIN: Don't I know you from somewhere?

WINCHELL: I've never been to Winnipeg before. I'm a foreigner.

MARTIN: From where?

WINCHELL: Don't you hear the accent? Jolly old England, obviously. I'll have a small Tom Collins.

MARTIN: They come in one size.

WINCHELL: Inconvenience.

MARTIN: And for dinner?

WINCHELL: I told you I'm full on bread.

MARTIN: You can't by law sit here and drink alcohol without ordering food.

WINCHELL: They do things strangely in your land. Why must I go by your laws?

MARTIN: I'm very sorry but my manager said if you don't order, I'll have to charge you $15 for all the bread you've eaten and ask you to leave.

WINCHELL: What an outrage.

MARTIN: You're sure we don't know each other?

WINCHELL: Just get me one more bread basket. Now. I'm the customer and I want bread.

MARTIN: The manager said—

WINCHELL: Then get me another waiter, someone with some pull.

            MIA walks in and sits alone at a table, WINCHELL is interested.

MARTIN: I don't need this in my life. Pay up and go.

WINCHELL: Just a second. Man to man. That woman there. I want to impress her.

MARTIN: OK.

WINCHELL: What shall I do?

MARTIN: Send her a bottle of wine?

WINCHELL: Send her a bottle of wine. Will that be acceptable to your manager?

MARTIN:	Sure. What kind?
WINCHELL:	Uh... Pino grigio. Hold on. *(Reads from notebook.)* Santa Margarita.
MARTIN:	Yes, sir.
WINCHELL:	Just a second.
MARTIN:	Sir?
WINCHELL:	How much is that?
MARTIN:	Uh, I think about $65.
WINCHELL:	Make it a glass.
MARTIN:	A glass of pinot.
WINCHELL:	Santa Margarita.
MARTIN:	I got that. Six ounce or 9?
WINCHELL:	Nine.
MARTIN:	Waiter?
WINCHELL & MARTIN:	Six.
MARTIN:	Right.
WINCHELL:	Just a second.
MARTIN:	Hmm?
WINCHELL:	What's the cheapest wine you have here by the glass?
MARTIN:	*(With dawning realization.)* The cheapest... Our house white is lovely.
WINCHELL:	I don't need to get her tipsy. I'm going to go over there and surprise her in a minute. Just send her a large six ounce.
MARTIN:	Would you like me to give her a message?

WINCHELL: Yes, tell her she has an admirer in the room.

MARTIN: Right away, Sir!

> *MARTIN exits. WINCHELL spies on MIA.*
> *MARTIN re-enters, brings MIA a glass of wine.*
> *MARTIN goes, re-enters and goes to MIA's table.*

              Can I get you anything else, madame?

MIA: Exactly what I had last night and the night before
              please.

MARTIN: I've got that right here, as you well know. Where
              would you like it?

> *WAITER turns to WINCHELL and gives him the*
> *A-OK gesture.*

MIA: In my room. Room service. And make sure it's hot.

MARTIN: You want to sign for that?

MIA: I'll sign for it.

MARTIN: Got enough ink in your pen?

MIA: I think I do.

MARTIN: I thought ladies in their sixties weren't supposed to
              have ink in their pens.

MIA: It all depends on what they're signing for. Can you
              get off early?

MARTIN: It's not looking good.

MIA: Frick my life.

MARTIN: I guess you're going to have to wait to get your
              dinner.

MIA: It better be nutritious.

MARTIN: You'll be stuffed, I promise you that. Your meal will

be chock full of vitamins, it'll be like the thickest
smoothie—

A bell dings.

Shit.

> *WAITER exits and comes on with food and a bottle
> of champagne.*

WINCHELL: I didn't want the drink, you fool, I thought you
understood… Champagne? That's not what I…
Lobster tails and shrimps?

MARTIN: An ice cold bottle of Veuve Clicqout, and the pride
of the Hotel Fort Garry—the Seafarer's platter, just
as you ordered, sir.

WINCHELL: I asked for the cheapest—

MARTIN: You said the Seafarer and champagne, no mistaking
it, and funny, those are the most expensive things
on the menu, and if you're going to make trouble
we're calling the police. You see my manager there
holding the phone? They'll put you in a jail cell.

WINCHELL: How much will it cost?

MARTIN: You're going to eat it and you're going to pay for
it.

> *MIA looks to see what's going on.*

What's the matter? Not hungry, sir? You want to
count the shrimps for a wrap up?

WINCHELL: Wha—?

MARTIN: You old bastard, you got me fired from my last job
over a shrimp and now you're going to sit here and
clean your plate and pay for it.

WINCHELL: That must have been my twin brother, not me! I'm
from England! *(Eats.)* Happy?

MARTIN: Delighted. We're watching you.

           WAITER goes to MIA's table.

           And do you have everything you desire, madame?

MIA: Far from it and you know it. What was all the hullaballoo? That man looks so familiar.

MARTIN: You get all kinds in here.

MIA: Surprising. It's so high end.

MARTIN: How high does your end get?

           WINCHELL packs up his food in a napkin and sneaks, then makes a break for it in a full out run out of the restaurant.

MIA: Is he supposed to be doing that?

           WAITER turns to see, then runs after WINCHELL.

MARTIN: Hey—get back here!

WINCHELL: Police! Assault! Police!

           WINCHELL throws lobster at MARTIN, upstage. MIA sits, oblivious, drinking wine.

Scene 3

           Next day. The Eames chairs are gone. Doorbell rings. RICHARD and WINCHELL at door.

RICHARD: (*Whispers.*) Give her the power, sir.

WINCHELL: Open the door, that's what you'll be paid to do if—

              MIA is let into the house by RICHARD.

              You're late.

MIA: I know.

RICHARD: Madame, what a pleasure to have you home again.

MIA: Save it, suck up. How are you, Winch?

RICHARD: Will that be all, sir?

WINCHELL: Yes, that will be all.

              RICHARD exits, mouthing, 'Be nice'.

              How wonderful to see you. What an expensive looking dress.

MIA: It's new. Aren't you going to invite me to sit down?

WINCHELL: I thought we'd look out at the garden, the light is so lovely. But you hardly need an invitation to do whatever you please here, exactly half of everything being yours.

MIA: It's a courtesy. This is no longer my home. I live at Hotel Fort Garry.

WINCHELL: Yes, yes, yes, you do live at the Hotel Fort Garry. You really do. I'm so glad about that. Chocolate fountains flowing every day. It's a great comfort to me to know you're comfortable.

              MIA chortles ironically.

              It must be just exquis— Mia, why of all places must you stay at the Hotel Fort Garry?!

MIA: To gall you, primarily.

WINCHELL: Well, you do. I mean, it's good you like it!

MIA: There are so many little things I don't miss about home. The way you won't oil the locks...

WINCHELL: I want to hear it if someone is sneaking in!

MIA: Are you going to offer me a drink?

WINCHELL: What will you have? Your great favourite, Pinot Grigio? Ha ha! And you think I don't notice things. Now, I'd like nothing more than to listen to you speak. How are you spending your days?

MIA: Lately, going over separation papers with my lawyer.

WINCHELL: Ah. Using a lawyer is a miserable business. They're keen and business-like, assure you they'll move heaven and earth, and then disappear for days at a time, only to emerge with an padded invoice!

MIA: Where did you find your lawyer—out of the yellow pages?

WINCHELL: Where else? After I made price comparisons, of course. Where did you find yours? Is he living year round at the Hotel Fort Garry? Ha ha!

MIA: Word of mouth.

WINCHELL: Well, what's the difference? It's all the same.

MIA: I'm not so sure. I was late today because my lawyer needed to bring something to my attention. I brought this along so you could clarify.

WINCHELL: Come, this is a dinner to meet Emily's new driftwood. Can't we leave all that behind for the time being?

MIA: Just one small thing about your assets.

WINCHELL: I'd rather talk about you.

MIA: *(With a document.)* You say your only assets are:
                'clothing and miscellaneous objects as set out in
                the following inventory and priced at the most
                fair valuation possible. Item—one four-poster bed
                complete with hangings of Hungarian lace, very
                handsomely worked upon in an olive-coloured
                material, together with six chairs, the whole in
                very good condition and lined in red and blue shot
                silk; item—one single bed with hangings of good
                Aumale serge in old rose with silk fringes and
                valance.'

WINCHELL: Well, yes, what of it?

MIA: Wait. 'Item—one set of hangings in tapestry
                representing the loves of Gombaut and Macea;
                items—one large table in walnut with twelve
                pedestal legs with draw-out leaf at either end and
                fitted underneath with six stools.'

WINCHELL: Confound it—so?

MIA: Patience please. 'Item—three muskets, inlaid in
                mother-of-pearl; item—one brick furnace with two
                retorts and three flasks, very useful for anyone
                interested in distilling; item—'

WINCHELL: Oh!

MIA: 'Item—one Bologna lute complete with strings
                or nearly so; item – one crocodile skin, three feet
                six inches in length and stuffed with hay, a very
                attractive curio for suspension from the ceiling—all
                the aforementioned articles are my assets valued at
                upwards of fourteen thousand dollars.' Winchell, is
                this the junk we found in the attic when we bought
                the house and couldn't sell at the yard sale? It is.
                Don't you blush at this list?

WINCHELL: Well, it is worth about fourteen thousand!

MIA: Balls to that! And most interestingly, we've noticed discrepancies between what the stores are bringing in and what is getting deposited in the joint account. What are you up to, Winch? My imagination is running wild.

WINCHELL: I...I...I don't believe I... Let's be civil. This is a party.

MIA: I thought I was getting some Pinot Margarita. Is it going to just materialize?

WINCHELL: Of course, your white wine.

MIA: Numbers don't lie, Winch. Everything can be traced.

WINCHELL: I wish it were so! I've made it my life's work keeping your wild spending on track, and those numbers can't be traced, so I won't get any credit for them in a divorce court, but anyway, you are, really, breathtakingly beautiful tonight, Mia, I'm compelled to say.

MIA: My wine?

WINCHELL: But of course.

WINCHELL is notating.

MIA: Stop right there. I am having that drink. God—I'll get it myself.

MIA exits. EMILY enters, despondent.

WINCHELL: Is your equilibrium failing again?

EMILY: He's an hour late.

WINCHELL: Perhaps he got waylaid at a weenie roast.

MIA: I love him Daddy.

WINCHELL: If one may judge from appearances, he may not return the feelings.

EMILY: You know what Daddy? Don't even.

EMILY exits. RICHARD enters with some soil on his face.

WINCHELL: How am I doing?

RICHARD: Beautifully, sir! Sublime! But I think now is the time for plan H for Honesty.

WINCHELL: Honesty? Are you sure that's necessary? I can leap to my plan.

RICHARD: Plan H, sir, oh, yes, sir, very much so—H.

WINCHELL: Wash your—

RICHARD: Thank you, sir.

RICHARD sees MIA coming back with her wine, and hurries off but not before MIA catches him.

MIA: If you water down any booze tonight, I'll have your balls, Richard.

RICHARD: Thank you, madame.

RICHARD exits.

MIA: Miss me?

WINCHELL: My dear, I've been doing some soul searching—

MIA: While I've been pouring wine?

WINCHELL: And well before. We have almost forty years to our credit. I love you, even if I haven't shown it as I should. One can get…off track in the love department in a long marriage. The business took over all our thoughts, didn't it? And then the child came unexpectedly. I admire you more than any woman I know. I'd hate for it to end like this. Won't you at least consider giving me another chance? I know I can be an outrageous fellow at times.

Perhaps you could tell me how you'd like me to act, and I'll do my best to listen.

MIA: Winch—Winch.

WINCHELL: My own little ball buster.

MIA: I've never heard you say you're wrong the years I've known you.

WINCHELL: And I haven't now.

MIA: Excuse me?

WINCHELL: I'm saying…circumstances can pull a good marriage down.

MIA: So you aren't saying you've been wrong about anything.

WINCHELL: I'm saying I'll do anything to save our marriage.

EMILY slouches in, mournful.

EMILY: Hi, Mommy.

MIA: Hey…where are my chairs?

WINCHELL: Oh, yes! Ugh—the old sciatica's playing up. I thought we'd try something kind of contemporary. Richard! Richard! Roll them in! Roll in the balls.

Four yoga balls roll in, via RICHARD. EMILY sits on one.

Very good for the back. I hope you'll bear with me.

MIA: Where are the Eames chairs you bastard?

EMILY: No, he's right. Weird—these are just like what we use at my yoga studio. They're great for the—

WINCHELL: The Eames chairs are safe in neutral territory.

MIA: I'm going to kill you.

EMILY: Why is no one on a ball except for Emily?

                WINCHELL and then MIA balance on yoga balls.

MIA: Where is he, Em?

EMILY: Late. OK? He's just a bit late.

WINCHELL: An hour and fifteen min--

EMILY: Don't count numbers, Daddy.

MIA: Why a girl as beautiful and thin as you would settle
                for—

EMILY: Don't start!

WINCHELL: Not a good sign when they're late.

MIA: It's the worst sign, actually.

WINCHELL: It signals a basic lack of—

EMILY: I've known plenty of turds who've been on time,
                OK? It doesn't mean squat.

                *RICHARD enters. He has soil on his hands and
                clothes.*

RICHARD: Sir, the dinner...

MIA: We are still waiting for a guest.

RICHARD: But—

MIA: What's the hurry, is this a fast food restaurant? Are
                we keeping you from something, Richard? Bring
                me a refresher.

WINCHELL: Richard, you may as well bring the watering can
                and water the plants while we wait—

MIA: Oh no you don't.

WINCHELL: What's the matter?

MIA: Don't you dare bring the watering can.

WINCHELL: He is my butler.

MIA: If he brings that can—

RICHARD: I'm sorry, sir, madame, but I'm afraid if I don't serve the dinner now it may go past the point of no return.

MIA: Oh, serve then, if you must.

RICHARD: Thank you, madame!

MIA: Will you stop calling me madame? It's getting on my nerves.

> *RICHARD exits.*

EMILY: Mommy, we can't eat before Martin gets here!

MIA: We've no choice. He can have a plate if he shows up.

EMILY: FML.

> *RICHARD enters with casserole and starts serving.*

MIA: Winchell, you do see your butler is filthy.

WINCHELL: What did I tell you about keeping clean?

RICHARD: Sir, I was picking radishes for supper.

MIA: Emily, are you growing radishes in your vegetable patch?

EMILY: Huh? No.

RICHARD: My mistake.

MIA: This isn't that old stew from the freezer.

WINCHELL: No! Richard insisted on cooking this from scratch, it's his mother's recipe.

MIA: Is that so, Richard?

RICHARD: Yes, ma'am.

MIA: How dare you ma'am me. I need more wine. ...And no one answered.

              All begin to eat, RICHARD stands by. EMILY picks at her food and then starts to cry.

WINCHELL: Buck up, girl.

MIA: Stop it, Em, you're being ridiculous.

EMILY: Why does everything work against me? Everything in the whole world conspires against me constantly. I have no luck. Absolutely no luck.

              MARTIN, dripping wet, passes by the window, sees them, and swings in through the window.

MARTIN: You never told me you had a pool.

WINCHELL: Uncle Jonathan's corn cob pipe.

MIA: Oh my god.

EMILY: Use a door much?

MARTIN: I think outside the box.

EMILY: Were you out back swimming the whole time?

MARTIN: I'm a Cancer. We're incapable of resisting a body of water.

MIA: Winchell...the waiter from the Italian restaurant. The one you stiffed. *(Aside.)* Or the one who stiffed me.

MARTIN: Hi Winch. Hi there, Mia.

EMILY: Mom, Dad, this is my fiancé Martin. Martin, this is Mia and…you can call him Winch. Everybody does. I sent you to the restaurant so you could meet him, he was going to tell you who he was at the end of the meal, but the plan didn't quite work.

MIA: And he's your fiancé? Emily, what an idiotic plan. I'm mortified, Otavio. I mean Martin. Have a seat. Where are your clothes?

MARTIN: By the pool.

MIA: Richard, would you be so kind? May I get you a drink, Martin? Our turn to serve you. I'm afraid we were just starting without you.

            RICHARD scoots to get the clothes.

MARTIN: I'd love a drink. Hey, that day you stiffed me? You made up for it.

EMILY: Huh?

MIA: Oh, please, don't—

MARTIN: Mia. She made up for it.

MIA: Please—! Pull up a ball and—

EMILY: Share my ball, baby.

            MARTIN shares EMILY's pilates ball.

MARTIN: She snuck back into the restaurant pretending she forgot her lipstick and slipped me a fifty.

WINCHELL: You hadn't forgot your lipstick?

MIA: Winch, what was I supposed to do? You force people to over-compensate for you!

WINCHELL: But the tip should have been no more than forty-two dollars! It's just plain extravagance!

MIA: I wasn't going to stand around asking him to make change after you'd humiliated us, was I?

MARTIN: I'm not complaining.

WINCHELL: I don't expect you are.

                WINCH flips back in his notebook and starts erasing.

MIA: What are you doing? It was my money, it's nothing to do with your tally.

WINCHELL: I don't care, you've just ruined that day.

                RICHARD enters with clothes.

MIA: Richard, see what you can do about warming up this food, will you? Let's start the party over.

WINCHELL: Yes, what she said, Richard.

                RICHARD clears up round one of the food, and takes everything away.

MIA: Winch, stop with the notebook. Martin, ha ha... Well! Tell us about yourself. Are you going to the university?

MARTIN: Not right now. I model sometimes. I'm basically serving and surfing. Meeting nice people, having good times with them.

WINCHELL: I thought only ladies modeled.

EMILY: Oh, no, Dad! They're called 'male models'.

WINCHELL: I stand corrected.

MIA: You say, 'not right now'. What will you study when the time comes?

MARTIN: Something I can make money at.

MIA: Modeling must pay well.

MARTIN: Yep, it sure does. It's the lifestyle—travel, everything catered, yoga, surfing, just spending my whole day keeping fit. Meeting interesting people…

MIA: I'm sure you do very well with it.

MARTIN: I do, thanks.

MIA: Very well indeed.

MARTIN: Yeah, I do.

MIA: It's not very long now you two have known each other, is it?

MARTIN: A month or two. Did someone mention a drink?

WINCHELL: I don't recall anyone bringing that up.

MIA: What will you have?

MARTIN: Whatever's going.

EMILY: Me too.

WINCHELL: Lovely weather for swimming, eh, Martin?

MARTIN: I'd like a place like this some day.

MIA: Thank you. We like it.

MARTIN: It reminds me of Rembrandt. I saw one of his when I was modeling in London.

MIA: Our house reminds you of Rembrandt?

WINCHELL: How so?

MARTIN: You know.

WINCHELL: Mia insisted on track lighting.

MIA: How does it remind you of Rembrandt?

MARTIN: Like a picture.

WINCHELL: You mean, a painting?

MIA: No, I think he means—are you saying our home is pretty as a picture?

MARTIN: Yeah.

MIA: Thank you, Martin.

WINCHELL: I see we'll need to speak very slowly and use words of one syllable.

      EMILY kicks WINCHELL in the shin.

OW-en Sound, Ontario!

MIA: Excuse me?

EMILY: Get the drinks, Dad.

WINCHELL: Certainly, my dear girl, daddy will get the drinks. Where's my butler? Butler? Richard!

EMILY: He's doing the dinner, Dad. Why don't you go?

WINCHELL: Rest assured, you can always count on me.

MIA: Then go, Winch.

WINCHELL: The butler should—

MIA: Go.

WINCHELL: Yes, Mia—whatever you say. Whatever you say.

      WINCHELL goes, muttering:

Someone just extended his probation by two weeks.

MIA: Darling, see that you father doesn't add any water, will you? Bring the bottle.

EMILY: OK, why don't you come with me, Martin? I can show you the house.

MARTIN:　Sure.

MIA:　No, no, leave him with me. We'll get acquainted.

EMILY:　That's sweet, Mom! OK!

>　*EMILY goes.*

MIA:　I hope I can rely on you.

MARTIN:　I'm discreet.

MIA:　You're discreet.

MARTIN:　Totally discreet. And nothing will change that.

MIA:　What do you mean?

MARTIN:　Nothing has to change when we get married, you know.

>　*Shouting offstage.*

EMILY:　*(Offstage.)* Daddy, let go!

WINCHE:　*(Offstage.)* No, you let go!

>　*EMILY and WINCHELL enter tussling over the wine bottle.*

EMILY:　Mom said to bring the bottle!

WINCHELL:　You never bring the bottle, you little fool! Watch and learn!

MIA:　I told her to bring the bottle.

WINCHELL:　Of course, my dear, you need only have said so! I would have brought the glass into the kitchen!

MARTIN:　As a server I can tell you, you never bring the glass to the bottle, you bring the bottle to the glass.

WINCHELL:　That all depends.

MIA:　I can't have been drinking from that bottle. It's full.

EMILY: I couldn't get to him in time.

MIA: My god, Winchell, you know how to irritate me!

WINCHELL: It was an accident! I spilled some water.

MARTIN: What's the problem?

MIA: Nothing, Martin. Wine and water spritzer.

WINCHELL: Where's my butler?

                RICHARD enters with casserole again.

RICHARD: Right here, sir! The food is re-heated.

WINCHELL: Pour my wife's wine.

EMILY: Doesn't he have enough to do?

MIA: I hope you didn't nuke that, Richard.

EMILY: Let's make a toast.

MIA: What shall we toast?

EMILY: Hello? Love and marriage.

MIA: If we must.

EMILY, MARTIN,
MIA &
WINCHELL: To love—

                Only EMILY and MARTIN finish the toast.

EMILY &
MARTIN: —and marriage.

WINCHELL: Let no man pull asunder.

MIA: Very sweet.

MARTIN: Isn't this gay?

                *RICHARD, serving the food, drops the casserole
                lid.*

WINCHELL: That comes out of your wages.

RICHARD: It didn't break.

WINCHELL: It comes out anyways.

RICHARD: Thank you, sir.

RICHARD serves MARTIN.

MARTIN: Thank you, Mr. Butler. This looks as good as lobster and champagne.

WINCHELL sputters.

MIA: Rather extravagant praise for an old chestnut stew.

All eat.

EMILY: Martin and I are very much in love.

MARTIN: Yeah.

MIA: I'm sure you are but don't you think this marriage is a bit... Winch, help me out here.

WINCHELL: Quick?

MIA: Drastic?

EMILY: I love him.

MIA: What's the rush to wed?

EMILY: We want the commitment.

MARTIN: We're in love.

MIA: Yes, we've got that, Martin, thank you.

EMILY: Mother—come on. Lighten up! You're on my side.

MIA: I'm sorry, no, not exactly. You whined for a dress and a trip and I gave in. But now I see—my god—

what a disservice I've done you all these years by spoiling you.

WINCHELL: It's what I've always warned you.

MIA: Shut up, Winchell. Please understand, Martin, this is my only child, my little girl. My baby.

MARTIN: She's your kid. I get it.

MIA: This marriage is all wrong. Emily, you're making the mistake of your life.

EMILY: Mom—no! Father believes in marriage, it's the most important thing to him. Dad?

MIA: Winch.

EMILY: Is marriage important, Dad?

MIA: Winchell.

WINCHELL: Marriage is...important to me.

MIA: Your father is saying that because he knows I'm about to clean him out in divorce court.

WINCHELL: Don't be hasty, Mia, we haven't tried couples therapy yet.

                 MIA sputters with surprise.

MIA: What'd you do with Winchell?

WINCHELL: I keep current.

MIA: You'd pay for couples therapy.

WINCHELL: We are Canadian. Surely it's covered.

EMILY: Can we get back to me? You've never once held me to an obligation, made me work, made me go to school. But I want commitment—not a new surf board. I'm not fooling around. Marriage is a holy sacrament, Mother!

MIA: Since when do you talk sacraments?

EMILY: Since now, OK? Dad? It's a sacrament, right?

WINCHELL: It...can be.

EMILY: Even Dad's on my side!

MIA: Why don't you speak up, Martin. Why do you want to get married so quickly?

MARTIN: I want to make a holy sacrament with her.

MIA: Right. This marriage is happening over my dead body!

EMILY: Mother, I'll never forgive you for this!

MIA: And what happens after your designer wedding, hmm? What will keep you in the style you're accustomed to? Ever heard of the word 'jobs'?

MARTIN: Funny you should ask, we wanted to talk to you about work.

WINCHELL: Hallelujah, she's moving out and going to work! Marriage is a holy sacrament!

WINCHELL begins notating in his book while MIA gives him a smack.

MIA: Where's your radar, Winch? Can't you see what's coming?

EMILY: Listen you guys, please just listen! We want you to set us up in the family business. We're not asking for anything but to work. We want to run the cafés. You're both retired now and your managers aren't even family! Martin has a really good point about that. Right honey? You can't know if they're really trustworthy if they're not family. Martin had a great idea. Let him run the cafés.

MIA: Go on. I'm fascinated.

EMILY: He's a waiter, he served you himself. He knows the business.

MIA: Waiters are trained monkeys. But our managers have proven themselves by years of loyal service. So we have a model/waiter, and you, whom I could barely get to take a shift a week in summer time— but cried because your allowance wasn't enough.

EMILY: I have to live on fifty dollars a week!

                WINCHELL sputters.

WINCHELL: You give her two hundred dollars a month—for bumming around?

MIA: It works out to that—sometimes.

WINCHELL: No wonder she won't work!

EMILY: I can barely afford pilates on what she gives me!

WINCHELL: Then get a job!

EMILY: OK, then let us run the business.

WINCHELL: Mia, you've created a monster.

MIA: I can give my daughter an allowance—it's my money!

EMILY: I have no life!

MIA: You know I want you to go to university, but you put me off. And now it's all my fault because I didn't force you. Fine. But now? You want us to turn over our businesses to you? You're in dreamland, miss!

                MIA exits.

MARTIN: *(To EMILY)* This isn't going off like you said.

                MARTIN follows MIA offstage.

EMILY: She won't listen, don't bother.

MARTIN: She'll listen to me.

               MARTIN exits.

EMILY: Can someone just please be happy for me getting
               married?

WINCHELL: You do take quite a risk in things turning out badly.
               But if you must you must. Of course, I won't pay
               out anymore than I have already. And you certainly
               won't run the businesses, no question about that.

EMILY: You said you believed in marriage. How can you
               just change your tune like that?

WINCHELL: I'm not changing my tune—go ahead, make your
               sacrament my dear. You're not a Scientologist—it's
               absolutely free.

EMILY: You're a cruel old miser, I hate you.

               EMILY exits. RICHARD follows her.

WINCHELL: Richard? Richard! Re-freeze the stew! We don't
               want to lose it now after all these years, man!

               WINCHELL notates his food cost savings.

Scene 4

               MARTIN and MIA, in an alcove.

MARTIN: Hold on there! Hey, I expected a little support from
               you back there.

               MARTIN kisses MIA.

               You know, I'd never done anything like that before,
               mother and daughter.

MIA: I find that hard to believe.

MARTIN: But you seemed like you needed a friend.

MIA: You knew that I was Emily's mother, but you…

MARTIN: But we'd never been officially introduced. There's a difference. But I really l like you now.

They get intimate for a moment.

Are you going to set us up in the business?

MIA: Never.

MARTIN: How would you like your husband and daughter to know about our little rendezvous?

MIA: If I lose my reputation, I won't miss it.

MARTIN: How about if you lose your daughter? Will you miss that?

MIA: Give me your hand, let me read your fortune. Hmm… Hmmm!

MIA slaps his face.

It doesn't look good.

MARTIN: Ouch!

MIA storms off. EMILY and RICHARD in another alcove.

EMILY: I'm going to lose Martin, Richard, I can see it in his eyes. He's vain and greedy.

RICHARD: You're right.

EMILY: I don't know why I love him.

RICHARD: I do. He's uncomplicated.

EMILY: My mother betrayed me. My father is useless.

RICHARD: I'm here for you! I've dug everywhere except—the petunia bed. It's got to be there! Dig—while I hold them off.

WINCHELL: (*Offstage.*) Richard! The stew, the stew, Richard, the stew! You must re-freeze the stew!

RICHARD: Go! Now!

EMILY: I'll do it!

RICHARD: Be careful, don't get caught.

EMILY: They owe me. I want that money.

> *EMILY rushes off and bumps into MARTIN.*

               I don't know what to say.

MARTIN: Start with, you're a liar. 'My folks'll pay for everything, we're rich.'

EMILY: I wanted to please you.

MARTIN: Nobody pleases me but me, get it? I was fending for myself when I was nine years old. People like your family really get me. Running around in your big houses, crying about nickels and dimes.

EMILY: What about us?

MARTIN: What about us?

EMILY: You realize you said you loved me back there?

MARTIN: I did?

EMILY: (*Aside.*) That's the first time he's said it.

MARTIN: (*Aside.*) Can I get a replay? (*To EMILY.*) So what about it?

EMILY: There's another way to get money, you know.

MARTIN: Such as?

EMILY: Just leave it to me. But first, I was thinking…

MARTIN: Yeah?

EMILY:　　　I thought of a new way we could do it.

MARTIN:　　How's that?

EMILY:　　　We could do it in the garden.

MARTIN:　　That's not a new way to do it.

EMILY:　　　It's a new place.

MARTIN:　　Doesn't qualify.

EMILY:　　　Well, I'd like to do it in the petunia bed—if you don't mind!

MARTIN:　　Mother's daughter.

EMILY:　　　Huh?

MARTIN:　　Bitchy. Both think you call the tune.

EMILY:　　　C'mon. Do me.

> *MARTIN and EMILY exit. WINCHELL wanders along, holding the stew, calling.*

WINCHELL:　Richard! Richard! The stew! The stew, man!

> *RICHARD and WINCHELL run into each other. RICHARD is carrying a huge crowbar and he hides it behind his back.*

RICHARD:　　I was looking everywhere for you, sir!

WINCHELL:　Were you indeed. I'm watching you, you know. I'm here—with the stew. If you don't freeze it now all with be lost.

RICHARD:　　God forbid we lose it, sir.

> *RICHARD takes the stew in one hand. WINCHELL looks out the window. EMILY can be seen from afar, humping motion.*

WINCHELL:　Richard, what is my daughter doing in the petunia bed? My prescription's a bit old.

RICHARD: She's working on a new vegetable patch.

WINCHELL: It looks oddly vigorous for gardening.

RICHARD looks out window and is momentarily taken aback.

RICHARD: They do gardening differently these days, sir. It's the new aerobics.

WINCHELL: More power to her. Seems to have died down now. She's gone down into the flowers. That's more the way we used to do it. What are you waiting for, man!? To the freezer!

RICHARD goes off, absentmindedly puts down the stew as he goes. RICHARD runs into MARTIN and they eat each others faces off.

MARTIN: Well?

RICHARD: I can't pick the locks, I can't break the locks, I can't persuade the locks. There's one from the 17th century!

MARTIN: I guess I marry the girl to get the money.

RICHARD: Why don't we just walk away. We have each other.

MARTIN: No chance. I'm enjoying this one.

RICHARD: She's a friend now.

MARTIN: You're never too young or too pretty to get a good duping.

RICHARD: Marty, you're not getting any younger. You're going to look pathetic in a few years.

Footsteps approach.

RICHARD: Oh, no!

RICHARD gives MARTIN the crowbar and he bolts. MIA enters with stew.

MIA: I found this on the bookshelf, butler. I believe you know what to do with it. Have you seen my daughter?

RICHARD: Third floor bathroom I believe.

MIA: Third floor? Lord. Thank you.

                  MIA exits. EMILY enters panting with the strongbox.

RICHARD: What's that?

EMILY: The strongbox!

RICHARD: The what?

EMILY: Hello the strongbox!

RICHARD: How'd you find the strongbox?

EMILY: It wasn't in the petunia bed. The money was inside the doghouse!

                  TOBY barks. EMILY and RICHARD look at each other, and then we hear WINCHELL begin to holler his following lines. RICHARD gestures to relieve EMILY of the strongbox and EMILY passes it to RICHARD in a panic, and RICHARD runs off. EMILY runs the other way. WINCHELL enters.

WINCHELL: Thieves! Conspirators! Robbers! Assassins! Murderers! Justice! Merciful heavens! I'm done for! I'm murdered! They've cut my throat; they've taken my money! Whoever can it be? Where's he gone to? Where is he now? Where is he hiding? How can I find him? Which way shall I go? Which way shan't I go? Is he here? Is he there? Stop! *(Catching his own arm.)* Give me back my money, you scoundrels! Ah, it's me! I'm going out of my mind! I don't know where I am or who I am or what I'm doing. Oh dear, my dear, darling money, my beloved, they've taken you away from me and now you are gone! I have lost my strength, my joy, and my consolation. It's all over for me. There's nothing left for me to do in the world! I can't go on living without you. It's the finish. I can't bear anymore. I'm dying, I'm dead, I'm buried! Will nobody bring me to life again by giving me my money or telling me who has taken it? Eh? What do you say? There's nobody there! Whoever did it must have watched his opportunity well and chosen the very moment I was entertaining guests! I must go. I'll demand justice! I'll have everyone in the house put to torture, manservant, daughter, fiancé and wife! Everyone—myself included! I suspect the whole pack of them!

MIA and then EMILY arrive to see what the fuss is.

WINCHELL: They both look like the thief to me! They're both in on it! My money is stolen! But where is the butler and the fiancé? Quickly! Catch them! Police! Judges! Hangmen! *(Aside.)* If I don't get my money back, I'll hang myself!

There is a rusty kind of squeak.

Back door!

MIA, EMILY, and WINCHELL run off, much ruckus, haul back MARTIN, wet from swimming.

MARTIN: What is this, the Spanish Inquisition?

WINCHELL: Why were you going out the back door?

MARTIN: To have a swim. Your family is bonkers.

EMILY: Daddy, are you sure your strongbox is gone?

MIA: What strongbox?

WINCHELL: I never said a strongbox was gone. So you're the thief, are you?

EMILY: Uh…yes…but not just me. Where's Richard. Richard?

                EMILY backs off and runs out.

MARTIN: Why don't you go and look again? I misplace things all the time.

MIA: I know you do. What's in this strongbox, Winchell?

WINCHELL: Private papers.

MIA: Oh, really?

MARTIN: Emily! Where are you?

                MARTIN moves to find her, and is restrained by WINCHELL.

WINCHELL: I'm not letting you out of my sight.

MARTIN: Hey, old timer, watch it, I'll knock your block off.

WINCHELL: Richard! Richard! I need you!

MARTIN: Emily! Get back here. We're going.

                Screams and a ruckus from without. EMILY and RICHARD enter, scrapping wildly. RICHARD is wearing a couture wedding dress and holding papers and the strongbox.

EMILY: My wedding dress! And what's this!? Two tickets to St. Bart's for you…and Martin?

WINCHELL: *(Taking the strongbox.)* Come to me, darling.

MIA: What?

EMILY: Richard? Are you marrying…Martin? Martin? How?

MARTIN: Do you need a description?

WINCHELL: To think of you taking advantage of my kindness and generosity. Getting yourself into my household on purpose to betray and play a trick like this.

RICHARD: I won't attempt to excuse or deny it.

WINCHELL: And in cahoots, the so-called fiancé, a...homosexual in disguise.

MARTIN: Not homo—2%.

EMILY: But...

RICHARD: Sorry, kid.

MARTIN: It's time you grew up, little girl.

MIA slaps MARTIN.

MIA: Don't you tell my daughter to grow up.

WINCHELL: This may be painful, Emily, but you have been saved.

MIA grabs the strongbox from WINCHELL.

MIA: What's in this strongbox, Winchell?

WINCHELL: It's just—some...money.

MIA: This is the money that's been siphoned off the business! You're a thief yourself. Half of this belongs to me! You're going to be sorry. I'm going to leave you in the poorhouse! I'm going to rake you over the—

WINCHELL: Not so fast! Now it's time for my plan! Plan WTF!

EMILY: WTF?

RICHARD: *(Aside.)* God protect us!

WINCHELL: I felt compelled to order a paternity test. *(Aside.)* Not cheap! *(Back.)* Plan WTF. Who's The Father?

MIA: How dare you?!

EMILY: A paternity test for me? Really? Well, come on!
                What did it say?

WINCHELL: I haven't opened it yet.

RICHARD: You haven't?! How can you stand it, sir?

WINCHELL: I'm not speaking to you, Richard, but since you ask,
                I'm not interested in these results unless Mia insists
                on pushing this to the hilt.

RICHARD: Gently, now. Madame! Sir! Think of the girl!
                Everyone! Watch what you're saying and doing!

MIA: I have an idea of what those tests cost, Winchell. I'm
                going to call your bluff. I don't think you've got a
                paternity test in there. Open it. I dare you.

                WINCHELL opens the envelope and reads.

MARTIN: Anybody taking bets?

                *RICHARD elbows MARTIN. WINCHELL passes
                it to EMILY as he speaks.*

WINCHELL: Let me tell you the story of a man. An innocent man,
                at sea in a marriage of betrayal! But he is washed up
                on good old terra firma. Our marriage is a lie—and
                therefore I'll have some leverage in court! Emily is
                not my biological daughter!

EMILY: You're not my biological father?

WINCHELL: *(Aside.)* I am not her biological father.

EMILY: *(Aside.)* He's not my biological father.

MIA: *(Aside.)* I knew that. *(Back.)* Winchell…Emmy….

RICHARD: Your daughter must not be used in a battle over
                money!

WINCHELL: Not a word from you, scoundrel!

EMILY: What do you care? Didn't you do the same?

MIA: And now you'll try to disinherit her, no doubt.

WINCHELL: Nonsense. Don't be alarmed, my daughter. My paternal affection for you is unchanged.

MIA: Oh really?

WINCHELL: I did have a hand in raising her, if you'll remember. My business is with you.

MIA: I can't believe you'd stoop to this.

WINCHELL: Let's not point fingers, shall we.

MIA: Winchell, I made a foolish mistake. But we got Emily out of it.

WINCHELL: Now, if we can amicably divorce, two Eames chairs each, and you leave my cashbox intact…

MARTIN: You people are too much.

EMILY: I don't want to hear a word out of you!

RICHARD: Emily, come here.

EMILY: No!

RICHARD: Come on, baby.

> *EMILY goes to RICHARD.*

EMILY: I didn't really save your life that day, did I? It was all a set up.

RICHARD: See, you are smart. But the point is, you thought you were saving my life. And for that I am just as grateful as if you had saved my life.

EMILY: I thought I sensed you paddling a bit there at the end. You're wearing my wedding dress.

MARTIN: Hey, what about my Armani suit?

RICHARD: Shut up, Marty. See, they were able to alter it after all. You have impeccable taste. Honey, Martin and I have been engaged for a year. I got there first. Give me hug—please.

EMILY reluctantly hugs RICHARD.

I'll spend my life making this up to you. But first let me get married in St. Bart's!

EMILY: I hate you. But I hate him more!

EMILY shoves MARTIN.

RICHARD: Me, too. He's eminently hatable. But we are getting married tomorrow.

MARTIN: We don't have any money now.

RICHARD: Shut your mouth, honey, I've worked too hard for this. Time to go.

RICHARD shoves MARTIN toward the door, but MARTIN swings back and kisses MIA.

MARTIN: I think I love you.

RICHARD: Go! What do you think you're doing? Go!

MARTIN: I'll go to St. Bart's—unless you've got a better idea.

RICHARD pulls MARTIN out the door, both men exit arguing:

RICHARD: You don't want to mess with me, I know too much—

MARTIN: You can't tame me no matter how hard you try.

RICHARD and MARTIN are gone.

EMILY: Mommy? Why did Martin says he loves you?

MIA: He's obviously a madman.

EMILY: I just lost my best friend and my fiancé. Mother? WTF?

WINCHELL: Good question. WTF?

MIA: Who's The Father? He was just a prime-of-life crisis. A waiter. A one night. It was nothing. I'll make this up to you both.

MIA hands WINCHELL the cashbox.

WINCHELL: My lovely cashbox…returned.

MIA: I should be running.

WINCHELL: What?

EMILY: Where?

MIA: Honey, Daddy does have a point. It's time to grow up, get a job, think about school. You've had lots of fun. Now it's Mommy's time to have fun, and I'm going to have some fun right now. Mommy's going to have the kind of fun that Mommy likes best. TTFN.

WINCHELL turns his back on her. MIA exits quickly.

WINCHELL: Never rely on anyone. Then you'll be self-sufficient and happy like me. So I take it you're not moving out then, eh? Very well.

WINCHELL flips to his notebook and begins erasing. He takes a paper out of his breast pocket, slides it over to her.

This is a lease for $650 a month. Sign it.

EMILY: It's not fair.

WINCHELL: Nobody's doing fair anymore. Sign it.

EMILY signs.

What do you think you'd like to do with your life?

EMILY: I have no idea.

WINCHELL: I hear that's what first year university is for. But I wouldn't know.

EMILY: University. FML.

> *WINCHELL opens the strongbox. It is empty. He digs through it and shakes it upside down in a panic. WINCHELL and EMILY look at each other.*

WINCHELL
& EMILY: The money!

WINCHELL: Gone.

EMILY: Oh, Daddy. No.

WINCHELL: My beautiful, gorgeous money.

> *WINCHELL is a broken man. Door bursts open. MIA, panting.*

Mia, they stole my—

> *MIA grabs a huge wad of bills from her handbag and fans herself with them.*

How did you—?

MIA: I knew they had it. I smelt it. No one is a match for me when it comes to sniffing out cold, hard cash.

WINCHELL: How true it is.

MIA: My, that was more fun than I've had in years!

EMILY: How did you get it off them?

MIA: They…won't be back.

MIA: What you've done, Winchell, embezzling this

money… It occurs to me. If we keep quiet—and fire our pesky accountant—no one will ever know this money existed. Which means no tax to the feds.

WINCHELL: So we split this? 50/50?

MIA: 60/40.

WINCHELL: 60/40?

MIA: Finder's fee.

WINCHELL: Why? Why do you always win? My god, you're beautiful right now. I could forgive you anything.

MIA: And I you.

WINCHELL: But I've done nothing wrong.

MIA: Never change, Winch.

WINCHELL: Nor you.

MIA: Darling, make no mistake about it—the very best times of my life have been with you

WINCHELL goes to kiss MIA.

Not the hair.

WINCHELL goes in for another kiss.

Not the dress.

WINCHELL goes in for one more kiss.

Lipstick! Now—about our Emily She spent her education fund, as I told you she would.

And she stole from us.

WINCHELL: A relentless pursuit of money.

MIA: She did have a good point, though.

WINCHELL: About our managers.

MIA: They could be skimming. You're going to have to pay rent now, Emily, just as your father said. So you'll go to work—full time in the cafés. What should she be?

WINCHELL: She did steal from us. Dishwasher?

MIA: Barista.

WINCHELL: Yes…almost as bad. This is what we'll want.

MIA: We want you to watch all of the staff. But particularly the managers. If someone eats a piece of cake for free, I want to hear about it.

WINCHELL: If someone takes a Coke, I want to know.

EMILY: So I'm like—a spy?

WINCHELL: Not like one.

MIA: You are one.

EMILY: That actually sounds fun. Yah! That sounds cool!

MIA: She's our daughter, Winch, as sure as I'm yours and you're mine.

> *Toby barks.*

> *Lights down.*

> *The End.*